T0301817

INDIAN
ECONOMY
Empirical Analysis on Monetary
and Financial Issues in India

INDIAN ECONOMY

Empirical Analysis on Monetary and Financial Issues in India

Takeshi Inoue

Nanzan University, Japan

Shigeyuki Hamori

Kobe University, Japan

 **World Scientific**

NEW JERSEY · LONDON · SINGAPORE · BEIJING · SHANGHAI · HONG KONG · TAIPEI · CHENNAI

Published by

World Scientific Publishing Co. Pte. Ltd.
5 Toh Tuck Link, Singapore 596224
USA office: 27 Warren Street, Suite 401-402, Hackensack, NJ 07601
UK office: 57 Shelton Street, Covent Garden, London WC2H 9HE

Library of Congress Cataloging-in-Publication Data
Inoue, Takeshi, 1973–
    Indian economy : empirical analysis on monetary and financial issues in India /
by Inoue Takeshi & Shigeyuki Hamori.
      pages cm
    Includes bibliographical references and index.
    ISBN 978-9814571906
    1. Monetary policy--India. 2. Finance--India. 3. Economic development--India. I. Hamori,
Shigeyuki, 1959–   II. Title.
    HG1235.I57 2015
    330.954--dc23

                                              2014008803

British Library Cataloguing-in-Publication Data
A catalogue record for this book is available from the British Library.

In-House Editors: Lum Pui Yee/Dipasri Sardar

Typeset by Stallion Press
Email: enquiries@stallionpress.com

Printed in Singapore

To Tadashi, Chieko, Sumiko, and Hideo
To Hitoshi, Makoto, and Naoko

Contents

About the Authors   xi

List of Figures   xiii

List of Tables   xv

List of Abbreviations   xvii

List of First Appearances   xix

Introduction   1

Part 1   Monetary Policy in India   7

Chapter 1.   An Empirical Analysis of the Money Demand Function in India   9

1.1   Introduction   9

1.2   Literature Review   11

1.3   Models   13

1.4   Data   14

1.5   Empirical Results   14

     1.5.1   Monthly data   14

     1.5.2   Annual data   19

1.6   Concluding Remarks   24

References   24

Chapter 2.   Financial Variables as Policy Indicators: Empirical Evidence from India   27

2.1   Introduction   27

2.2   Literature Review   29

2.3 Empirical Technique 30
2.4 Data 31
2.5 Empirical Results 32
2.6 Concluding Remarks 35
References 37

**Chapter 3. Is India Ready to Adopt a Policy Framework
Targeting Inflation?**   39

3.1 Introduction 39
3.2 Literature Review 40
3.3 Models 41
3.4 Data 42
3.5 Empirical Techniques 43
3.6 Empirical Results 44
    3.6.1 Simple Taylor rule 44
    3.6.2 Open economy Taylor rule 46
3.7 Concluding Remarks 48
References 48

Part 2   Financial Markets in India   **51**

**Chapter 4. Causal Relationships in Mean and Variance
between Stock Returns and Foreign
Institutional Investment in India**   53

4.1 Introduction 53
4.2 Literature Review 55
4.3 Empirical Technique 58
4.4 Data 61
4.5 Empirical Results 62
    4.5.1 Causality test based on the LA-VAR 62
    4.5.2 Causality test based on the CCF approach 64
4.6 Concluding Remarks 69
References 72

**Chapter 5. Market Efficiency of Commodity Futures
in India**   73

5.1 Introduction   73
5.2 Literature Review   75
5.3 Model   77
5.4 Empirical Techniques   77
5.5 Data   78
5.6 Empirical Results   80
    5.6.1 Full-sample analysis   80
    5.6.2 Sub-sample analysis   81
5.7 Concluding Remarks   82
References   83

**Chapter 6. What are the Sources of Real and Nominal
Exchange Rate Fluctuations? Evidence
from SVAR Analysis for India**   87

6.1 Introduction   87
6.2 Data   89
6.3 Empirical Technique   90
6.4 Empirical Results   92
    6.4.1 Results for India and the United States   92
    6.4.2 Results for India and the euro area   94
6.5 Concluding Remarks   95
References   96

**Part 3 Financial Development and Poverty Alleviation
in India**   99

**Chapter 7. How Has Financial Deepening Affected
Poverty Reduction in India?**   101

7.1 Introduction   101
7.2 Literature Review   104
7.3 Data   108
7.4 Models   112
7.5 Empirical Results   113

7.5.1 Results for the whole country   113
7.5.2 Results for the urban areas   115
7.5.3 Results for the rural areas   117
7.5.4 Summary   118
7.6 Concluding Remarks   119
References   122

**Chapter 8.   Financial Inclusion and Poverty Alleviation
                in India**   127

8.1 Introduction   127
8.2 A History of Financial Inclusion in India   128
8.3 Financial Inclusion and Poverty Conditions   132
8.4 Literature Review   136
8.5 Models and Data   138
8.6 Empirical Results   141
8.7 Concluding Remarks   143
References   144

**Chapter 9.   Concluding Remarks: Monetary Policy
                and Financial Sector for Sustainable
                Economic Growth and Poverty Reduction**   147

Index   153

About the Authors

Takeshi INOUE is an Associate Professor of Policy Studies at Nanzan University in Japan. He received his PhD from Kobe University. He previously worked as Research Fellow at Institute of Developing Economies (IDE-JETRO). His research interests include empirical analysis of Indian macroeconomy and finance-poverty nexus in developing countries.

Shigeyuki HAMORI is a Professor of Economics at Kobe University in Japan. He received his PhD from Duke University and has published many papers in refereed journals. He is the author or co-author of An Empirical Investigation of Stock Markets: the CCF Approach (Kluwer Academic Publishers, 2003), Hidden Markov Models: Applications to Financial Economics (Springer, 2004), Empirical Techniques in Finance (Springer, 2005), and Introduction of the Euro and the Monetary Policy of the European Central Bank (World Scientific, 2009). He is also the co-editor of Global Linkages and Economic Rebalancing in East Asia (World Scientific, 2013) and Financial Globalization and Regionalism in East Asia (Routledge, 2014).

List of Figures

3.1	Output Gap	43
4.1	Cumulative Net FII and Stock Price Index	54
4.2	Cumulative Net FII and Stock Price Index in Real Terms	55
5.1	Total Value of Commodities and Stocks in India (Rs. Billion)	74
5.2	The Movements of Commodity Price Indices	79
6.1	The Movements of the Effective Exchange Rates	88
8.1	Population Group-wise Distribution of Commercial Bank Branches (Number)	133
8.2	Population Group-wise Distribution of Credit Accounts (Accounts in Thousands)	134
8.3	Population Group-wise Distribution of Deposit Accounts (Accounts in Thousands)	135
8.4	Population Group-wise Distribution of Percentage of Population below the Poverty Line (% of Persons)	136

List of Tables

1.1   Cointegration Tests ($M1$, Monthly Data)   15

1.2   DOLS ($M1$, Monthly Data, Model 1)   16

1.3   DOLS ($M1$, Monthly Data, Model 2)   17

1.4   Cointegration Tests ($M2$, Monthly Data)   17

1.5   DOLS ($M2$, Monthly Data, Model 1)   18

1.6   DOLS ($M2$, Monthly Data, Model 2)   18

1.7   Cointegration Tests ($M3$, Monthly Data)   19

1.8   Cointegration Tests ($M1$, Annual Data)   20

1.9   DOLS ($M1$, Annual Data, Model 1)   20

1.10   DOLS ($M1$, Annual Data, Model 2)   21

1.11   Cointegration Tests ($M2$, Annual Data)   21

1.12   DOLS ($M2$, Annual Data, Model 1)   22

1.13   DOLS ($M2$, Annual Data, Model 2)   23

1.14   Cointegration Tests ($M3$, Annual Data)   23

2.1   Causality During the MIA Period
(April 1998 to June 2009)   33

2.2   Causality During the Monetary Targeting Period
(April 1985 to March 1998)   34

2.3   Causality During the MIA Period
(April 1998 to June 2009)   35

2.4   Causality During the Monetary Targeting Period
(April 1985 to March 1998)   35

3.1   Cointegration Tests (Simple Taylor Rule)   45

3.2   Cointegrating Regression (Simple Taylor Rule)   45

3.3   Cointegration Tests (Open Economy
Taylor Rule)   46

3.4 Cointegrating Regression (Open Economy
     Taylor Rule)   47
4.1 Causality from LA-VAR ($d_{max} = 1$)   63
4.2 Causality from LA-VAR ($d_{max} = 2$)   64
4.3 Empirical Results of the AR-EGARCH Model
     (January 1, 1999 to April 30, 2003)   66
4.4 Empirical Results of the AR-EGARCH Model
     (May 1, 2003 to March 31, 2008)   67
4.5 Causality in the Mean between FII Flows
     and Stock Returns   68
4.6 Causality in the Variance between FII Flows
     and Stock Returns   70
5.1 Unit Root Tests   79
5.2 Cointegration Tests   80
5.3 Cointegration Estimation Results
     (Full-sample Analysis)   81
5.4 Cointegration Estimation Results
     (Sub-sample Analysis)   82
6.1 Forecast Error Variance Decomposition
     (India and the United States)   93
6.2 Forecast Error Variance Decomposition
     (India and the Euro Area)   94
7.1 Summary of Literature on the Finance-
     Poverty Nexus   107
7.2 Definition and Sources of Each Variable   109
7.3 Financial Deepening and Poverty: Whole Country   114
7.4 Financial Deepening and Poverty: Urban Areas   116
7.5 Financial Deepening and Poverty: Rural Areas   117
7.6 Summary of Empirical Results   118
8.1 Number of Indebted Households (Number in Lakhs) . . .   131
8.2 Outstanding Household Debt
     (Amount in Rs. Crores)   132
8.3 Definition and Sources of Each Variable   140
8.4 Empirical Results   142

List of Abbreviations

ADF	augmented Dickey–Fuller
AIC	Akaike Information Criterion
AIDIS	All India Debt and Investment Survey
AR-EGARCH	AR-exponential GARCH
BSE	Bombay Stock Exchange
CCF	cross-correlation function
CRR	cash reserve ratio
DOLS	dynamic OLS
EGARCH	exponential GARCH
FII	foreign institutional investment
FMC	Forward Markets Commission
FMOLS	fully modified OLS
GARCH	Generalized Autoregressive Conditional Heteroscedasticity
GDP	gross domestic product
GMM	generalized method of moments
GOI	Government of India
IMF	International Monetary Fund
IPI	industrial production index
KCCs	Kisan Credit Cards
LAF	liquidity adjustment facility
LA-VAR	lag-augmented vector autoregression
MCX	Multi Commodity Exchange of India
MIA	multiple indicator approach
MOCAFPD	Ministry of Consumer Affairs, Food and Public Distribution

MOSPI	Ministry of Statistics and Programme Implementation
MSF	marginal standing facility
NCDEX	National Commodity and Derivatives Exchange
NEER	nominal effective exchange rate
NSDP	Net State Domestic Product
NSSO	National Sample Survey Organization
OLS	ordinary least squares
RBI	Reserve Bank of India
REER	real effective exchange rate
RRB(s)	Regional Rural Bank(s)
SBIC	Schwarz Bayesian Information Criterion
SBLP	Self-Help Group (SHG)-Bank Linkage Program
SEBI	Securities and Exchange Board of India
SLR	statutory liquidity ratio
SVAR	structural vector autoregression
VAR	vector autoregression
VMA	vector moving average
WPI	wholesale price index

List of First Appearances

Chapter 1

Inoue, T., Hamori, S., 2009. An empirical analysis of the money demand function in India. *Economics Bulletin* 29(2), 1225–1246.

Chapter 4

Inoue, T., 2009. The causal relationships in mean and variance between stock returns and foreign institutional investment in India. *Margin: The Journal of Applied Economic Research* 3(4), 319–337.

Chapter 5

Inoue, T., Hamori, S., 2014. Market efficiency of commodity futures in India. *Applied Economics Letters* 21(8), 522–527.

Chapter 6

Inoue, T., Hamori, S., 2009. What explains real and nominal exchange rate fluctuations?: Evidence from SVAR analysis for India. *Economics Bulletin* 29(4), 2810–2822.

Chapter 7

Inoue, T., Hamori, S., 2012. How has financial deepening affected poverty reduction in India? *Applied Financial Economics* 22(5), 395–408.

(Reprinted by permission of the publisher (Taylor & Francis Ltd, http://www.tandf.co.uk/journals).)

Chapter 8

Inoue, T., 2011. Financial inclusion and poverty alleviation in India: An empirical analysis using state-wise data, in: Hirashima, S., Oda, H., Tsujita, Y. (Eds.), *Inclusiveness in India: A Strategy for Growth and Equality*. Palgrave Macmillan, Basingstoke and New York, pp. 88–108.

Introduction

After launching the reforms of economic liberalization in the early 1990s, India entered a high-growth phase in the early 2000s. Every year since 2007, India has ranked third in Asia (after China and Japan) in terms of gross domestic product (GDP). Although the growth rate has been slowing down since 2011, India is expected to drive the global economy in the medium to long run. Meanwhile, according to the World Bank's estimate in 2008, the global number of poor living on less than USD 1.25 per day (2005 purchasing power parity prices) is approximately 1.4 billion, one-third of whom are concentrated in India, thus making it a country with the largest poor population (Chen and Ravallion, 2008).

This book is composed of empirical studies on monetary and financial issues related to economic growth and poverty reduction in India. The broad structure of this book is as follows. Part 1 is about the characteristics and changes in monetary policy since the 1990s, Part 2 discusses the recent developments in financial markets, and Part 3 deals with the contribution of financial development toward poverty reduction since the 1970s.

Part 1 (comprising Chapters 1–3) analyzes India's monetary policy, with a special focus on the policy framework. With the ultimate goal of stabilizing the price level and promoting economic growth, since the mid-1980s, India had employed monetary targeting by considering the growth rate of the broadly defined money (M3) as its intermediate target. However, against the backdrop of financial sector reforms in the 1990s, there were increasing concerns that money demand would become unstable and that the relationship between money supply and price, which underlies monetary targeting, would weaken in India (Mohan, 2008), as was the case with other emerging countries that adopted monetary targeting (Inoue *et al.*, 2013). Consequently, in 1998, India's central bank, the Reserve Bank of India

(RBI), switched the monetary policy framework from monetary targeting to the multiple indicator approach (MIA), which monitors a variety of macroeconomic variables as policy indicators to draw future perspectives for policy objectives.

Chapter 1 discusses whether such a change in the monetary policy framework of India was appropriate. Specifically, by using the cointegration test and the dynamic ordinary least squares (DOLS), we test the long-run stability of the money demand function and examine the effectiveness of monetary targeting as a policy framework and the appropriateness of its transition to MIA. Then, Chapter 2 analyzes the effectiveness of MIA, which has been functioning as a policy framework since 1998. For the analysis, we perform the Granger causality test by using the vector autoregression (VAR) model to examine whether the macroeconomic variables monitored under the MIA are useful in predicting the movements of the output and price levels. Next, Chapter 3 estimates India's monetary policy reaction function on the basis of the Taylor rule by using the DOLS. Here, we investigate the effect of short-term interest rate on inflation rate and examine whether India is ready to adopt the inflation-targeting type of policy framework.

Part 2 (composed of Chapters 4–6) analyzes the issues related to the Indian financial markets. Chapter 4 discusses the stock market, which has a long history as the first stock exchange was established in 1875, much before India's independence. Although the Indian stock market has observed mostly consistent price increases since 2003 when the economy began its high growth, it has also shown volatile movements especially since early 2008. We focus on the investment trends among foreign investors as one of the factors that cause such fluctuations in stock prices and analyze the relationship between stock returns and foreign institutional investment in Indian equities from 1999 to 2008 by applying the cross-correlation function approach.

Chapter 5 covers the commodity futures market. Similar to the stock market, commodity futures trading has a long history in India. However, unlike the case of the stock market, the government had intervened repeatedly to prohibit trades in the commodity market. Yet, as the government lifted the prohibition against futures trading in all commodities in 2003 and established national-level multi-commodity exchanges over the last decade, the commodity futures market witnessed a surge in volumes and prices during this period. Owing to these changes, the commodity market has grown to become one of the major financial markets in India. In this chapter, we estimate the long-term relationship between the spot price and future price in the commodity market from 2006 to 2011 by using cointegration test, the DOLS method, and the fully modified OLS method, and examine market efficiency of the expanding commodity futures market.

At the end of Part 2, Chapter 6 examines the foreign exchange market. Here, an empirical analysis is conducted to assess the factors causing the exchange-rate fluctuations in India. In the literature, there is an argument that in order to increase external competitiveness, the central bank in India does attempt to maintain the real exchange rate at a desirable level, as other developing countries do (Kohli, 2003; Jha, 2008), although the RBI itself has not formally acknowledged it. To address this, by applying a VAR model and using monthly data from 1999 to 2009, we analyze the sources of shock that causes exchange rate fluctuations and verify whether it is appropriate for India to set a real exchange rate as a goal.

Part 3 discusses the nexus between finance and poverty in India. According to the Indian government, the poverty ratio was steadily decreasing in the country between FY 1973 and FY 2004; however, the number of the poor has remained approximately at 300 million during this time period, accounting for about one-quarter of India's current total population. Having achieved high growth in the last decade, eliminating poverty has become a pressing issue for India. In this regard, in Part 3, we analyze whether and how financial development has contributed to poverty alleviation in India between FY 1973 and FY 2004 from the following viewpoints.

There have been a number of theoretical and empirical studies on financial development (e.g., King and Levine, 1993; Demetriades and Hussein, 1996; Demirgüç-Kunt and Maksimovic, 1996; Levine and Zervos, 1998; Luintel and Khan, 1999; Kirkpatrick, 2000; Apergis *et al.*, 2007). In these studies, financial development is typically referred to as "financial deepening" and is perceived as the increased scale of the financial sector in the real economy. These studies have empirically demonstrated that financial deepening contributes to economic growth through various channels and that there is a positive, bidirectional causal relationship between financial deepening and economic growth. In recent years, on the premise of the close relationship between these two variables, studies are underway to determine

whether financial deepening is effective in reducing poverty among a large
number of countries. Referencing these latest studies, Chapter 7 measures
financial depth as the ratio of credit or deposits of the scheduled commercial
banks to GDP, and examines the effect of financial deepening on poverty
reduction in India by using state-level panel data.

Since the late 1960s, the Indian government has successively implemented various initiatives to expand formal banking services to rural areas,
where impoverished people are concentrated. With the onset of economic
liberalization in the early 1990s, systematic financial sector reforms that
placed substantial emphasis on the efficiency and profitability of the banking system were implemented. As a result, the state-controlled initiatives
to expand the outreach of banking facilities and credit supply to rural
areas temporarily slowed down. However, in 2004, the Indian government
announced "inclusive growth" as a slogan for spreading the benefits of
economic growth to everyone including the poor. Since then, the emphasis
has been placed on ensuring access to and usage of basic formal banking
services to all people at an affordable cost. This is called "financial inclusion" and has received a great deal of attention as of late. Therefore, in
Chapter 8, we measure the progress of financial inclusion by the number
of bank branches and bank accounts, and examine the role of each measure
in the process of financial development toward reducing poverty in India.

Chapter 9 summarizes the conclusion of every previous chapter and
recommends changes to the monetary and exchange rate policy and the
financial sector in India to help it realize sustainable economic growth and
poverty reduction in the future.

This book is the fruition of our collaborative research, and some parts
have been published in *Applied Economics Letters, Applied Financial Economics, Economics Bulletin, Margin: The Journal of Applied Economic
Research*, and *Inclusiveness in India*. Although the chapters published in
these journals and the book have undergone considerable revision upon
becoming chapters of this book, we would like to express our greatest
appreciation to each publisher of the journals and the book for kindly per-
mitting us to include these as chapters in this book. In addition, we truly
appreciate Ms. Pui Yee Lum at World Scientific Publishing and Ms. Dipasri
Sardar at Academic Consulting and Editorial Services for their tremendous
assistance in editing and publishing this book.

Finally, it would not have been possible for us to prepare and publish this book without the support from our families. We would like to dedicate this book to our family members, who constantly support our research activities.

References

Apergis, N., Filippidis, I., Economidou, C., 2007. Financial deepening and economic growth linkages: A panel data analysis. *Review of World Economics* 143, 179–198.

Chen, S., Ravallion, M., 2008. The developing world is poorer than we thought, but no less successful in the fight against poverty. World Bank Policy Research Working Paper 4703, The World Bank, Washington, DC.

Demetriades, P.O., Hussein, K.A., 1996. Does financial development cause economic growth? Time-series evidence from 16 countries. *Journal of Development Economics* 51, 387–411.

Demirgüç-Kunt, A., Maksimovic, V., 1996. Financial constraints, uses of funds, and firm growth: An international comparison. World Bank Policy Research Working Paper 1671, The World Bank, Washington, DC.

Inoue, T., Toyoshima, Y., Hamori, S., 2013. Inflation targeting in South Korea, Indonesia, the Philippines, and Thailand: The impact on business cycle synchronization between each country and the world, in: Kinkyo, T., Matsubayashi, Y., Hamori, S. (Eds.), *Global Linkages and Economic Rebalancing in East Asia*. World Scientific, Singapore, pp. 85–108.

Jha, R., 2008. Inflation targeting in India: Issues and prospects. *International Review of Applied Economics* 22, 259–270.

King, R., Levine, R., 1993. Finance and growth: Schumpeter might be right. *The Quarterly Journal of Economics* 108, 717–737.

Kirkpatrick, C., 2000. Financial development, economic growth, and poverty reduction. *The Pakistan Development Review* 39, 363–388.

Kohli, R., 2003. Real exchange rate stabilisation and managed floating: Exchange rate policy in India, 1993–2001. *Journal of Asian Economics* 14, 369–387.

Levine, R., Zervos, S., 1998. Stock markets, banks and economic growth. *American Economic Review* 88, 537–558.

Luintel, K.B., Khan, M., 1999. A quantitative reassessment of the finance-growth nexus: Evidence from a multivariate VAR. *Journal of Development Economics* 60, 381–405.

Mohan, R., 2008. Monetary policy transmission in India. *BIS Papers 35*. Bank for International Settlements, Basel, 259–307.

Part 1

Monetary Policy in India

Chapter 1

An Empirical Analysis of the Money Demand Function in India

1.1 Introduction

India's financial sector was first deregulated in the mid-1980s, when measures, such as introducing 182-day treasury bills, lifting the call money interest-rate ceiling, and establishing certificates of deposits and commercial paper, were taken in order to increase the efficiency of the government securities market as well as that of the money market (Sen and Vaidya, 1997). Furthermore, in the wake of the balance of payments crisis in 1991, there began an intermittent series of more systematic financial sector reforms that continues today. For example, the reform of the Indian interest-rate structure, which had previously been strictly managed by the Reserve Bank of India (RBI), began with the April 1992 deregulation of deposit rates, and this has progressed to the point where commercial banks are now permitted to freely set all rupee lending rates and their deposit rates above Rs. 1 lakh.[1,2] The above are just a few examples of how interest-rate structure deregulation and the introduction of new financial products have progressed in India over the past 20 years.

Moreover, before the reforms, the RBI had long been constrained by the government's fiscal management practices. For instance, governmental budget deficits were mainly financed by the central bank through

---

[1] A lakh is equal to one hundred thousand (100,000).
[2] Except for savings bank deposits up to Rs. 100,000, interest rates for resident Indians have been greatly deregulated.

the issuance of 91-day ad hoc Treasury bills as well as the pre-emption of commercial banks' resources under the statutory liquidity ratio (SLR) requirement. Additionally, monetary expansion that emanated from deficit financing was accommodated by an increase in the cash reserve ratio (CRR) requirement.[3] As a part of the financial reforms, however, in September 1994, the RBI agreed to limit the issuance of 91-day bills, which were finally eliminated in April 1997. At the same time, the CRR and SLR have also gradually been reduced, with the former now used as a complementary operating instrument. As a result, the RBI has reined in the automatic monetization of budget deficits and has successfully increased its operational independence in monetary policy management matters.

Theoretical research and empirical analyses, primarily using data on developed countries, have shown that the money demand function can become unstable as a result of such financial innovations and financial sector reforms. Partly because of instability in the money demand function, many central banks have in recent years switched from money supply targeting, which is focused on monetary aggregates as the intermediate target, to inflation targeting, which seeks to stabilize prices by adjusting interest rates based on inflation forecasts. In 1998, the RBI abandoned its flexible monetary targeting approach in favor of the multiple indicator approach (MIA), ending the use of money supply as the intermediate target, but retaining it as an important indicator of future prices. Consequently, examining the characteristics of the money demand function of India's financial sector, which has undergone significant changes since the 1980s, should offer significant implications for the RBI's present and future monetary policy. This study, therefore, uses annual data for the period 1976–2007 and monthly data for the period January 1980–December 2007 in order to estimate and describe India's money demand function, which is derived from real money balances, interest rates, and output.

The remainder of this chapter is organized as follows. We begin by reviewing the relevant research and discussing the unique contributions

---

[3]The SLR is a prescribed proportion of net demand and time liabilities, which banks are required to invest in government and other approved securities, whereas the CRR is a prescribed proportion of net demand and time liabilities, which banks are required to hold in the form of cash balances with the RBI.

of our study. In Section 1.3, the models are presented and in Section 1.4, variables are defined, sources are provided, and data characteristics are explained. In Section 1.5, we perform cointegration tests using both monthly and annual data, examine the long-term stability of the money demand function, and use the dynamic ordinary least squares (DOLS) (Saikkonen, 1992; Stock and Watson, 1993) method to examine the sign conditions and significance of output and interest-rate coefficients. Lastly, the analytical results are presented to discuss the characteristics of India's money demand function and implications for its monetary policy.

1.2 Literature Review

India's money demand function has been the subject of numerous quantitative research efforts. The first study to explicitly consider the stationarity of, and cointegration relationships among, the variables of the money demand function was presented by Moosa (1992), which used three types of money supply — cash, M1, and M2 — to perform cointegration tests on real money balances, short-term interest rates, and industrial production from 1972 to 1990. Moosa's (1992) results indicated that for all three types of money supply, money balance had a cointegrating relationship with output and interest rates. However, greater numbers of cointegrating vectors were detected for cash and M1 than for M2, leading the author to state that narrower definitions of money supply are preferable for pursuing monetary policy.

Bhattacharya (1995), like Moosa (1992), considered three types of money supply — M1, M2, and M3 — and used annual data from 1950 to 1980 to analyze India's money demand function. By performing cointegration tests for real money balances, real gross national product, and long-term and short-term interest rates, the author detected a cointegrating relationship among variables only when money supply was defined as M1 and clearly showed that long-term interest rates are more sensitive to money demand than are short-term interest rates. In addition, Bhattacharya (1995), after estimating an error correction model based on the cointegration test results, found that the error correction term is significant and negative in the case of M1 and that monetary policy is stable in the long term when money supply is narrowly defined.

In the same vein, Bahmani-Oskooee and Rehman (2005) analyzed the money demand functions for India and six other Asian countries during 1972–2000. Using the autoregressive distributed lag approach described in Pesaran *et al.* (2001), they performed cointegration tests on real money supplies, industrial production, inflation rates, and exchange rates (versus the US dollar). For India, cointegrating relationships were detected for M1, but not for M2, leading them to conclude that M1 is the appropriate money supply definition to use when setting monetary policy.

In contrast to the above, some previous research has used a broad definition of money supply to hold that India's money demand function is stable. In one example, Pradhan and Subramanian (1997) employed cointegration tests and an error correction model, and using annual data for 1960 to 1994, detected relationships among real money balances, real gross domestic product (GDP), and nominal interest rates. By estimating an error correction model using M1 and M3 as money supply definitions, they found the error correction term to be significant and negative, thereby confirming that the money demand function is stable for both M1 and M3.

Das and Mandal (2000) considered only the M3 money supply in stating that India's money demand function is stable. They used monthly data between April 1981 and March 1998 to perform cointegration tests and detected cointegrating vectors among money balances, industrial production, short-term interest rates, wholesale prices, share prices, and real effective exchange rates. Their position, therefore, was that long-term money demand relevant to M3 is stable. Similarly, Ramachandran (2004) also considered only the M3 money supply in using annual data for the period of FY 1951 to FY 2000 to perform cointegration tests on nominal money supply, output, and price levels. Because stable relationships were discovered among these three variables, the author stated that an increase in M3 in the long-term can be used as a latent indicator of future price movements.

The foregoing review suggests that previous research tends to find that India's money demand function is stable.[4] Further, studies carried out using multiple money supply definitions have tended to conclude that because India's money demand function is more stable when money supply is

---

[4] Nag and Upadhyay (1993), Parikh (1994), Rao and Shalabh (1995), Rao and Singh (2006), among others, also performed quantitative analyses of India's money demand function.

defined narrowly, the central bank should adopt cash or M1 as the narrow definition of money supply when determining monetary policy. In stark contrast, other studies have concluded that the money demand function is stable when money supply is broadly defined. Views on what definition of money supply to use for monetary policy, therefore, differ.

Given these different definitions of money supply, this study uses both monthly and annual data, considers three types of money supply, namely M1, M2, and M3, and comprehensively estimates India's money demand functions for each case. We also discuss the implications of the empirical results for the formulation of the RBI's monetary policy. In contrast to previous studies, however, after performing cointegration tests on money supply, output, and interest rates as the money demand function variables, this study applies the DOLS and describes India's money demand function by examining the sign conditions and statistical significance of the variable coefficients.

1.3 Models

Of the various theories of this topic, Kimbrough (1986a, 1986b) and Faig (1988) derived the following money demand function by explicitly considering transaction costs:

$$\frac{M_t}{P_t} = L(Y_t, R_t), \quad L_Y > 0, \quad L_R < 0, \tag{1}$$

where M_t represents nominal money supply for period t, P_t represents the price index for period t, Y_t represents output for period t, and R_t represents the nominal interest rate for period t. Increases in output bring about increases in money demand, while increases in interest rates decrease money demand.

We can thus use two models corresponding to Equation (1) in order to conduct an empirical analysis.

Model 1: $\ln(M_t) - \ln(P_t)$

$$= \beta_0 + \beta_1 \ln(Y_t) + \beta_2 R_t + u_t, \quad \beta_1 > 0, \quad \beta_2 < 0. \tag{2}$$

Model 2: $\ln(M_t) - \ln(P_t)$

$$= \beta_0 + \beta_1 \ln(Y_t) + \beta_2 \ln(R_t) + u_t, \quad \beta_1 > 0, \quad \beta_2 < 0. \tag{3}$$

Equations (2) and (3) are both log linear models, but the former uses the level of interest rates and the latter uses the logarithm value of interest rates.

1.4 Data

For monthly data, we used data of the period January 1980–December 2007. The data source for the industrial production index (IPI) (seasonally adjusted by X12) and the wholesale price index (WPI) was the International Financial Statistics published by the International Monetary Fund (IMF). We obtained M1, M2, and M3 from various issues of the RBI Monthly Bulletin. We deflated these monetary aggregates by the WPI and used the call rate as the interest rate. The call rate was obtained from RBI (2006) from January 1980 to December 2005 and from RBI (2007a, 2008) from January 2006 to December 2007.

For annual data, we used data of the period 1976–2007. Real GDP and the GDP deflator were taken from IMF (2008). As before, we obtained M1, M2, and M3 from various issues of the RBI Monthly Bulletin. We deflated these monetary aggregates by the GDP deflator and again used the call rate as the interest rate. The call rate was obtained from RBI (2007b, 2008). Logarithm values were used for money supply, price levels, and output (industrial production and GDP). Finally, interest rates were analyzed in two ways, namely by taking a logarithm in one case and not in the other.

As a preliminary analysis, we carried out the augmented Dickey–Fuller tests for the logs of real money balances, output, and interest rates (Dickey and Fuller, 1979). As a result, the level of each variable was found to have a unit root, whereas the first difference of each variable was found to not have a unit root. Thus, we can state that each variable is non-stationary with a unit root.

1.5 Empirical Results

1.5.1 Monthly data

First, we analyzed the money demand function in relation to the use of $M1$ using the monthly data over the period January 1980–December 2007. For that analysis, we conducted Johansen cointegration tests for the money demand function (Johansen and Juselius, 1990; Johansen, 1991). There are

Table 1.1   Cointegration Tests ($M1$, Monthly Data)

Model	Hypothesized Number of Cointegration Equations	Maximum Eigenvalue Test	Trace Test
Model 1	0	60.889*	75.573*
	At most 1	13.937	14.684
	At most 2	0.747	0.747
Model 2	0	62.636*	77.424*
	At most 1	14.073	14.788
	At most 2	0.716	0.716

Note: * indicates that the null hypothesis is rejected at the 5% significance level.

two kinds of Johansen-type tests: the trace test and the maximum eigen-value test.

Table 1.1 shows the results of the cointegration tests for Model 1 and Model 2. Model 1 includes the logs of real money balances, the logs of industrial production, and the interest rate, whereas Model 2 includes the logs of real money balances, of industrial production, and of interest rates. Table 1.1 states that the null hypothesis of no cointegrating relation is rejected at the 5% significance level for both models. As the existence of the cointegrating relation was supported, we thus estimated the money demand function using the DOLS.

When we estimate the cointegrating vector, we cannot use the ordinary least squares (OLS). Although the OLS estimator of the coefficients of coin-tegrating regression is consistent, the non-normal distribution of error terms means that the tests carried out may yield an invalid statistical inference (Agbola and Damoense, 2005, p. 152). To overcome this problem, we used the DOLS and estimated the cointegating vector by adding ΔY_t and ΔR_t, and their leads and lags.[5]

Table 1.2 shows the estimation results with respect to Model 1. As is evident from this table, the output coefficient is significant and positive (1.148 for $K = 1$, 1.150 for $K = 2$, and 1.156 for $K = 6$), whereas the interest-rate coefficient is significant and negative (-0.004 for $K = 1$, -0.005 for $K = 2$, and -0.005 for $K = 6$). Thus, the sign condition

---

[5] Standard errors were calculated using the method of Newey and West (1987).

Table 1.2   DOLS ($M1$, Monthly Data, Model 1)

$$\log(m1_t) - \log(p_t) = \beta_0 + \beta_1 \log(y_t) + \beta_2 r_t + \sum_{i=-K}^{K} \gamma_{yi} \Delta \log(y_t) + \sum_{i=-K}^{K} \gamma_{ri} \Delta r_t + u_t$$

Lead and Lag	Variable	Coefficient	SE	t-Statistic	p-value	$\bar{R}^2$
$K = 1$	Constant	2.953	0.074	39.861	0.000	0.991
	$\log(y_t)$	1.148	0.016	72.494	0.000	
	r_t	−0.004	0.001	−3.542	0.001	
$K = 2$	Constant	2.948	0.063	47.070	0.000	0.992
	$\log(y_t)$	1.150	0.014	85.220	0.000	
	r_t	−0.005	0.001	−4.084	0.000	
$K = 6$	Constant	2.913	0.054	54.074	0.000	0.995
	$\log(y_t)$	1.156	0.011	108.258	0.000	
	r_t	−0.005	0.002	−3.392	0.001	

Notes: (1) SE is the Newey–West heteroskedasticity and autocorrelation consistent (HAC) Standard Error (lag truncation = 5).
(2) y is the IPI, and r is the interest rate.

of the money demand function holds for all cases. Table 1.3 presents the estimation results with respect to Model 2, showing that the sign condition of the money demand function holds for all cases. The output coefficient is significant and positive (1.143 for $K = 1$, 1.144 for $K = 2$, and 1.148 for $K = 6$), while the interest-rate coefficient is significant and negative (−0.048 for $K = 1$, −0.055 for $K = 2$, and −0.060 for $K = 6$). Hence, a cointegrating relation is supported and the existence of a money demand function with respect to $M1$ is statistically supported.

Next, we considered the money demand function when using $M2$ for the money supply component. Table 1.4 indicates the results of the cointegration tests for Model 1 and Model 2, showing that the null hypothesis of no cointegration is rejected at the 5% significance level for both models. As before, because the existence of the cointegrating relation was supported, we estimated the money demand function using the DOLS. Table 1.5 shows the estimation results with respect to Model 1. As is evident from this table, the sign condition of the money demand function holds. The output coefficient is significant and positive (1.097 for $K = 1$, 1.098 for $K = 2$, and 1.102 for $K = 6$), while the interest-rate coefficient is significant and

Table 1.3   DOLS ($M1$, Monthly Data, Model 2)

$\log(m1_t) - \log(p_t)$

$$= \beta_0 + \beta_1 \log(y_t) + \beta_2 \log(r_t) + \sum_{i=-K}^{K} \gamma_{yi} \Delta \log(y_t) + \sum_{i=-K}^{K} \gamma_{ri} \Delta \log(r_t) + u_t$$

Lead and Lag	Variable	Coefficient	SE	t-Statistic	p-value	$\bar{R}^2$
$K = 1$	Constant	3.036	0.089	33.952	0.000	0.991
	$\log(y_t)$	1.143	0.016	69.662	0.000	
	$\log(r_t)$	−0.048	0.013	−3.572	0.000	
$K = 2$	Constant	3.045	0.076	40.304	0.000	0.992
	$\log(y_t)$	1.144	0.014	82.829	0.000	
	$\log(r_t)$	−0.055	0.013	−4.321	0.000	
$K = 6$	Constant	3.025	0.066	46.202	0.000	0.995
	$\log(y_t)$	1.148	0.010	109.878	0.000	
	$\log(r_t)$	−0.060	0.014	−4.143	0.000	

Notes: (1) SE is the Newey–West HAC Standard Error (lag truncation = 5).
(2) y is the IPI, and r is the interest rate.

Table 1.4   Cointegration Tests ($M2$, Monthly Data)

Model	Hypothesized Number of Cointegration Equations	Maximum Eigenvalue Test	Trace Test
Model 1	0	25.333*	39.305*
	At most 1	11.831	13.972
	At most 2	2.141	2.141
Model 2	0	26.296*	39.635*
	At most 1	11.045	13.340
	At most 2	2.295	2.295

Note: * indicates that the null hypothesis is rejected at the 5% significance level.

negative (−0.005 for $K = 1$, −0.006 for $K = 2$, and −0.006 for $K = 6$). Table 1.6 presents the estimation results with respect to Model 2, showing that the sign condition of the money demand function holds. The output coefficient is significant and positive (1.091 for $K = 1$, 1.091 for $K = 2$, and 1.093 for $K = 6$), while the interest-rate coefficient is significant and negative (−0.054 for $K = 1$, −0.062 for $K = 2$, and −0.069 for

Table 1.5   DOLS ($M2$, Monthly Data, Model 1)

$$\log(m2_t) - \log(p_t) = \beta_0 + \beta_1 \log(y_t) + \beta_2 r_t + \sum_{i=-K}^{K} \gamma_{yi} \Delta \log(y_t) + \sum_{i=-K}^{K} \gamma_{ri} \Delta r_t + u_t$$

Lead and Lag	Variable	Coefficient	SE	t-Statistic	p-value	$\bar{R}^2$
$K = 1$	Constant	3.213	0.076	42.297	0.000	0.990
	$\log(y_t)$	1.097	0.017	66.593	0.000	
	r_t	−0.005	0.001	−3.951	0.000	
$K = 2$	Constant	3.210	0.066	49.010	0.000	0.991
	$\log(y_t)$	1.098	0.014	76.741	0.000	
	r_t	−0.006	0.001	−4.521	0.000	
$K = 6$	Constant	3.182	0.058	54.554	0.000	0.994
	$\log(y_t)$	1.102	0.012	94.582	0.000	
	r_t	−0.006	0.002	−3.828	0.000	

Notes: (1) SE is the Newey–West HAC Standard Error (lag truncation = 5).
(2) y is the IPI, and r is the interest rate.

Table 1.6   DOLS ($M2$, Monthly Data, Model 2)

$$\log(m2_t) - \log(p_t)$$
$$= \beta_0 + \beta_1 \log(y_t) + \beta_2 \log(r_t) + \sum_{i=-K}^{K} \gamma_{yi} \Delta \log(y_t) + \sum_{i=-K}^{K} \gamma_{ri} \Delta \log(r_t) + u_t$$

Lead and Lag	Variable	Coefficient	SE	t-Statistic	p-value	$\bar{R}^2$
$K = 1$	Constant	3.307	0.091	36.158	0.000	0.990
	$\log(y_t)$	1.091	0.017	64.229	0.000	
	$\log(r_t)$	−0.054	0.014	−3.899	0.000	
$K = 2$	Constant	3.318	0.079	42.139	0.000	0.991
	$\log(y_t)$	1.091	0.015	74.904	0.000	
	$\log(r_t)$	−0.062	0.013	−4.636	0.000	
$K = 6$	Constant	3.308	0.070	47.239	0.000	0.994
	$\log(y_t)$	1.093	0.011	96.265	0.000	
	$\log(r_t)$	−0.069	0.015	−4.602	0.000	

Notes: (1) SE is the Newey–West HAC Standard Error (lag truncation = 5).
(2) y is the IPI, and r is the interest rate.

Table 1.7   Cointegration Tests ($M3$, Monthly Data)

Model	Hypothesized Number of Cointegration Equations	Maximum Eigenvalue Test	Trace Test
Model 1	0	20.403	27.351
	At most 1	5.217	6.947
	At most 2	1.730	1.730
Model 2	0	19.409	25.935
	At most 1	5.098	6.527
	At most 2	1.429	1.429

Note: * indicates that the null hypothesis is rejected at the 5% significance level.

$K = 6$). Hence, as before, a cointegrating relation is supported, while the existence of a money demand function with respect to $M2$ is also statistically supported.

Finally, we considered the money demand function when using $M3$. Table 1.7 indicates the results of the cointegration tests for Model 1 and Model 2. As is evident from this table, the null hypothesis (in which there is no cointegrating relation) is not rejected at the 5% significance level for either of the models. Hence, a cointegrating relation is not supported, while the existence of a money demand function with respect to $M3$ is also not statistically supported.

1.5.2   Annual data

We also analyzed the money demand function in relation to the use of $M1$ using the annual data over the period 1976–2007. The fact that industrial production does not necessarily reflect total output in the Indian economy makes it worthwhile analyzing the money demand function using annual data, (that is, GDP data). Table 1.8 presents the results of the cointegration tests for Model 1 and Model 2, showing that the null hypothesis of no cointegrating relation is rejected at the 5% significance level for both models. As the existence of the cointegrating relation was supported, we estimated the money demand function using the DOLS. Table 1.9 shows the estimation results with respect to Model 1. Here, the output coefficient is significant and positive (1.004 for $K = 1$, 0.981 for $K = 2$, and 0.977 for $K = 3$), whereas the interest-rate coefficient is significant and negative

Table 1.8   Cointegration Tests ($M1$, Annual Data)

Model	Hypothesized Number of Cointegration Equations	Maximum Eigenvalue Test	Trace Test
Model 1	0	29.038*	40.371*
	At most 1	8.891	11.333
	At most 2	2.442	2.442
Model 2	0	31.294*	42.740*
	At most 1	8.936	11.446
	At most 2	2.511	2.511

Note: * indicates that the null hypothesis is rejected at the 5% significance level.

Table 1.9   DOLS ($M1$, Annual Data, Model 1)

$$\log(m1_t) - \log(p_t) = \beta_0 + \beta_1 \log(y_t) + \beta_2 r_t + \sum_{i=-K}^{K} \gamma_{yi} \Delta \log(y_t) + \sum_{i=-K}^{K} \gamma_{ri} \Delta r_t + u_t$$

Lead and Lag	Variable	Coefficient	SE	t-Statistic	p-value	$\bar{R}^2$
$K = 1$	Constant	4.041	0.294	13.750	0.000	0.972
	$\log(y_t)$	1.004	0.077	13.064	0.000	
	r_t	−0.037	0.010	−3.700	0.001	
$K = 2$	Constant	3.822	0.167	22.907	0.000	0.994
	$\log(y_t)$	0.981	0.045	21.922	0.000	
	r_t	−0.026	0.006	−4.482	0.001	
$K = 3$	Constant	3.758	0.131	28.638	0.000	0.995
	$\log(y_t)$	0.977	0.047	20.786	0.000	
	r_t	−0.024	0.005	−5.019	0.001	

Notes: (1) SE is the Newey–West HAC Standard Error (lag truncation = 5).
(2) y is real GDP, and r is the interest rate.

(-0.037 for $K = 1$, -0.026 for $K = 2$, and -0.024 for $K = 3$). Thus, the sign condition of the money demand function holds for all cases. Table 1.10 indicates the estimation results with respect to Model 2, showing that the sign condition of the money demand function holds for all cases. The output coefficient is significant and positive (1.002 for $K = 1$, 1.001 for $K = 2$, and 1.062 for $K = 3$), while the interest-rate coefficient is significant and

Table 1.10   DOLS ($M1$, Annual Data, Model 2)

$\log(m1_t) - \log(p_t)$

$$= \beta_0 + \beta_1 \log(y_t) + \beta_2 \log(r_t) + \sum_{i=-K}^{K} \gamma_{yi} \Delta \log(y_t) + \sum_{i=-K}^{K} \gamma_{ri} \Delta \log(r_t) + u_t$$

Lead and Lag	Variable	Coefficient	SE	t-Statistic	p-value	$\bar{R}^2$
$K = 1$	Constant	4.490	0.388	11.586	0.000	0.974
	$\log(y_t)$	1.002	0.077	12.987	0.000	
	$\log(r_t)$	−0.340	0.087	−3.895	0.001	
$K = 2$	Constant	4.088	0.259	15.777	0.000	0.994
	$\log(y_t)$	1.001	0.052	19.103	0.000	
	$\log(r_t)$	−0.232	0.062	−3.777	0.002	
$K = 3$	Constant	3.897	0.152	25.607	0.000	0.994
	$\log(y_t)$	1.062	0.045	23.841	0.000	
	$\log(r_t)$	−0.238	0.053	−4.468	0.002	

Notes: (1) SE is the Newey–West HAC Standard Error (lag truncation = 5).
(2) y is real GDP, and r is the interest rate.

Table 1.11   Cointegration Tests ($M2$, Annual Data)

Model	Hypothesized Number of Cointegration Equations	Maximum Eigenvalue Test	Trace Test
Model 1	0	29.447*	40.292*
	At most 1	8.943	10.846
	At most 2	1.903	1.903
Model 2	0	31.869*	42.697*
	At most 1	8.929	10.828
	At most 2	1.899	1.899

Note: * indicates that the null hypothesis is rejected at the 5% significance level.

negative (−0.340 for $K = 1$, −0.232 for $K = 2$, and −0.238 for $K = 3$). Thus, a cointegrating relation is supported, while the existence of a money demand function with respect to $M1$ is statistically supported.

Next, we considered the money demand function when using $M2$. Table 1.11 indicates that the null hypothesis of no cointegration is rejected at

Indian Economy

Table 1.12   DOLS (*M*2, Annual Data, Model 1)

$$\log(m1_t) - \log(p_t) = \beta_0 + \beta_1 \log(y_t) + \beta_2 r_t + \sum_{i=-K}^{K} \gamma_{yi} \Delta \log(y_t) + \sum_{i=-K}^{K} \gamma_{ri} \Delta r_t + u_t$$

Lead and Lag	Variable	Coefficient	SE	*t*-Statistic	*p*-value	$\bar{R}^2$
$K = 1$	Constant	4.367	0.289	15.132	0.000	0.968
	$\log(y_t)$	0.940	0.076	12.367	0.000	
	r_t	−0.040	0.010	−4.064	0.001	
$K = 2$	Constant	4.161	0.165	25.223	0.000	0.994
	$\log(y_t)$	0.917	0.044	20.729	0.000	
	r_t	−0.030	0.006	−5.139	0.000	
$K = 3$	Constant	4.101	0.131	31.284	0.000	0.995
	$\log(y_t)$	0.913	0.048	19.119	0.000	
	r_t	−0.028	0.005	−5.721	0.000	

Notes: (1) SE is the Newey–West HAC Standard Error (lag truncation = 5).
(2) *y* is real GDP, and *r* is the interest rate.

the 5% significance level for both Models 1 and 2. Table 1.12 then presents the estimation results with respect to Model 1 using the DOLS, showing that the sign condition of the money demand function holds. The output coefficient is significant and positive (0.940 for $K = 1$, 0.917 for $K = 2$, and 0.913 for $K = 3$), while the interest-rate coefficient is significant and negative (−0.034 for $K = 1$, −0.030 for $K = 2$, and −0.028 for $K = 3$). Table 1.13 then shows the estimation results with respect to Model 2, demonstrating that the sign condition of the money demand function holds. Here, the output coefficient is significant and positive (0.938 for $K = 1$, 0.937 for $K = 2$, and 0.999 for $K = 3$), while the interest-rate coefficient is significant and negative (−0.367 for $K = 1$, −0.265 for $K = 2$, and −0.272 for $K = 3$). Hence, a cointegrating relation is supported, while the existence of a money demand function with respect to *M*2 is also statistically supported.

Finally, we considered the money demand function when using *M*3. Table 1.14 shows that the null hypothesis (no cointegrating relation) is not rejected at the 5% significance level in three out of four cases, implying that a cointegrating relation may not be supported; in other words, the existence

Table 1.13   DOLS ($M2$, Annual Data, Model 2)

$\log(m1_t) - \log(p_t)$

$$= \beta_0 + \beta_1 \log(y_t) + \beta_2 \log(r_t) + \sum_{i=-K}^{K} \gamma_{yi} \Delta \log(y_t) + \sum_{i=-K}^{K} \gamma_{ri} \Delta \log(r_t) + u_t$$

Lead and Lag	Variable	Coefficient	SE	t-Statistic	p-value	$\bar{R}^2$
$K = 1$	Constant	4.851	0.379	12.806	0.000	0.970
	$\log(y_t)$	0.938	0.076	12.385	0.000	
	$\log(r_t)$	−0.367	0.086	−4.281	0.000	
$K = 2$	Constant	4.469	0.256	17.484	0.000	0.994
	$\log(y_t)$	0.937	0.051	18.357	0.000	
	$\log(r_t)$	−0.265	0.061	−4.317	0.001	
$K = 3$	Constant	4.286	0.156	27.550	0.000	0.994
	$\log(y_t)$	0.999	0.046	21.556	0.000	
	$\log(r_t)$	−0.272	0.054	−5.021	0.001	

Notes: (1) SE is the Newey–West HAC Standard Error (lag truncation = 5).
(2) y is real GDP, and r is the interest rate.

Table 1.14   Cointegration Tests ($M3$, Annual Data)

Models	Hypothesized Number of Cointegration Equations	Maximum Eigenvalue Test	Trace Test
Model 1	0	20.722	31.414*
	At most 1	6.712	10.692
	At most 2	3.980	3.980
Model 2	0	18.044	28.319
	At most 1	6.516	10.274
	At most 2	3.758	3.758

Note: * indicates that the null hypothesis is rejected at the 5% significance level.

of a money demand function with respect to $M3$ may not be statistically supported.

In summary, our empirical results using annual data are consistent with those using monthly data. Thus, the cointegrating relation for the money demand function is statistically supported for $M1$ and $M2$, but not for $M3$ based on the results derived from both monthly and annual data.

1.6 Concluding Remarks

If an equilibrium relationship is observed in the money demand function, financial authorities are able to employ appropriate money supply controls in order to maintain a reasonable inflation rate. Against this background, this chapter empirically analyzed India's money demand function from 1980 to 2007 using monthly data and from 1976 to 2007 using annual data. The presented results support the existence of an equilibrium relation in money demand when money supply is defined as M1 or M2, but no such relation when money supply is defined as M3. Because these results were obtained for both monthly and annual data, the findings are concluded to be unaffected by data intervals and robust in this setting.

These findings suggest a number of implications for monetary policy in India. In the mid-1980s, the RBI adopted monetary targeting that focused on the medium-term growth rate of the M3 money supply. Monetary targeting was used as a flexible policy framework to be adjusted in accordance with changes in production and prices rather than as a strict policy rule. However, amid ongoing financial innovations and financial sector reforms, the RBI announced in 1998 that it would be switching to the MIA in order to be able to consider a wider array of factors when setting policy. Under this new policy framework, the M3 growth rate is used as a reference indicator.

In general, a reference indicator, as an indicator of future economic conditions, is used as something between an operating instrument and a final objective, and no target levels are set, as is the case, for example, with intermediate targets. However, in India, in spite of being used as a reference indicator, the growth rate forecast for M3 is publicly announced on an annual basis and thus it serves as a measure of future price movements. Consequently, Indian financial authorities, despite having changed their policy framework, continue to pay significant attention to M3 movements. The empirical results of this chapter, by contrast, suggest that it would be more appropriate for the RBI to control price levels by referring to M1 and M2, rather than M3, when managing monetary policy.

References

Agbola, F.W., Damoense, M.Y., 2005. Time-series estimation of import demand functions for pulses in India. *Journal of Economic Studies* 32, 146–157.

Bahmani-Oskooee, M., Rehman, H., 2005. Stability of the money demand function in Asian developing countries. *Applied Economics* 37, 773–792.

Bhattacharya, R., 1995. Cointegrating relationships in the demand for money in India. *The Indian Economic Journal* 43, 69–75.

Das, S., Mandal, K., 2000. Modeling money demand in India: Testing weak, strong and super exogeneity. *Indian Economic Review* 35, 1–19.

Dickey, D.A., Fuller, W.A., 1979. Distribution of the estimators for autoregressive time series with a unit root. *Journal of the American Statistical Association* 74, 427–431.

Faig, M., 1988. Characterization of the optimal tax on money when it functions as a medium of exchange. *Journal of Monetary Economics* 22, 137–148.

International Monetary Fund (IMF), 2008. *International Financial Statistics, April.* IMF, Washington, D.C.

Johansen, S., 1991. Estimation and hypothesis testing of cointegration vectors in Gaussian vector autoregressive models. *Econometrica* 59, 1551–1580.

Johansen, S., Juselius, K., 1990. Maximum likelihood estimation and inference on cointegration — With applications to the demand for money. *Oxford Bulletin of Economics and Statistics* 52, 169–210.

Kimbrough, K.P., 1986a. Inflation, employment, and welfare in the presence of transactions costs. *Journal of Money, Credit and Banking* 18, 127–140.

Kimbrough, K.P., 1986b. The optimum quantity of money rule in the theory of public finance. *Journal of Monetary Economics* 18, 277–284.

Moosa, I., 1992. The demand for money in India: A cointegration approach. *The Indian Economic Journal* 40, 101–115.

Nag, A.K., Upadhyay, G., 1993. Estimating money demand function: A cointegration approach. Reserve Bank of India Occasional Papers 14, Reserve Bank of India, Mumbai, 47–66.

Newey, W., West, K., 1987. A simple positive semi-definite, heteroskedasticity and autocorrelation consistent covariance matrix. *Econometrica* 55, 703–708.

Parikh, A., 1994. An approach to monetary targeting in India. Reserve Bank of India Development Research Group Study 9, Reserve Bank of India, Mumbai.

Pesaran, M.H., Shin, Y., Smith, R.J., 2001. Bounds testing approaches to the analysis of level relationships. *Journal of Applied Econometrics* 16, 289–326.

Pradhan, B.K., Subramanian, A., 1997. On the stability of the demand for money in India. *The Indian Economic Journal* 45, 106–117.

Ramachandran, M., 2004. Do broad money, output, and prices stand for a stable relationship in India? *Journal of Policy Modeling* 26, 983–1001.

Rao, B.B., Shalabh, 1995. Unit roots cointegration and the demand for money in India. *Applied Economics Letters* 2, 397–399.

Rao, B.B., Singh, R., 2006. Demand for money in India: 1953–2003. *Applied Economics* 38, 1319–1326.

Reserve Bank of India (RBI), 2006. *Handbook of Monetary Statistics of India.* RBI, Mumbai.

Reserve Bank of India (RBI), 2007a. *Macroeconomic and Monetary Developments First Quarter Review 2007–08.* RBI, Mumbai.

Reserve Bank of India (RBI), 2007b. *Handbook of Statistics on Indian Economy 2006–07.* RBI, Mumbai.

Reserve Bank of India (RBI), 2008. *Macroeconomic and Monetary Developments in 2007–08.* RBI, Mumbai.

Reserve Bank of India (RBI), various issues. *RBI Monthly Bulletin.* RBI, Mumbai.

Saikkonen, P. 1992. Estimation and testing of cointegrated systems by an autoregressive approximation. *Econometric Theory* 8, 1–27.

Sen, K., Vaidya, R.R., 1997. *The Process of Financial Liberalization.* Oxford University Press, Delhi.

Stock, J.H., Watson, M.W., 1993. A simple estimator of cointegrating vectors in higher order integrated systems. *Econometrica* 61, 783–820.

Chapter 2

Financial Variables as Policy Indicators:
Empirical Evidence from India

2.1 Introduction

In India, the preamble of the Reserve Bank of India (RBI) Act sets out the central bank's objectives as being "to regulate the issue of the bank notes and the keeping of reserves with a view to securing monetary stability in India and generally to operate the currency and credit system of the country to its advantage." These objectives have been generally interpreted as referring to price stability and economic growth, and they have remained the same since the enactment of this act in 1934, though their relative emphasis has changed depending on the prevailing circumstances (Reddy, 2005, p. 222). In contrast, the conduct of the monetary policy in India has undergone significant changes.

In terms of operating instruments of monetary policy, during the 1990s, the RBI gradually shifted emphasis from direct instruments such as the cash reserve ratio (CRR) to market-based instruments, and expanded the array at its command. For instance, in April 1997, the RBI reactivated the bank rate by linking it to all other interest rates and now uses it to signal the medium-term stance of monetary policy. Moreover, the RBI implemented open market sales to sterilize the monetary impact of the capital inflow surge in the latter half of the 1990s, and in June 2000, introduced a full-fledged liquidity adjustment facility (LAF) to modulate day-to-day liquidity conditions.[1] A series of these indirect instruments is available following the deregulation of the administered interest rate structure, development of a government securities market, and increased integration of different financial markets.

Furthermore, because of financial sector reforms and the resultant financial liberalization, the central bank's monetary policy framework underwent an evolution. From 1985 to 1998, the RBI adopted flexible monetary targeting focused on M3 growth as the intermediate target. Under monetary targeting, reserve money was used as the operating target controlled by bank reserves through the CRR. However, as financial deregulation increased, it was increasingly felt that financial innovations and technology had systematically eroded the predictive potential of money demand estimations relative to the past (Mohan, 2008, p. 260), although empirical studies generally point out the stability of money demand functions in India, as reviewed in Chapter 1. Accordingly, the RBI thought it necessary to monitor a set of additional variables as indicators for policy formulation, while money supply continued to serve as an important information variable (Kannan *et al.*, 2006, p. 70).

Finally, in April 1998, the RBI formally announced a policy framework shift from monetary targeting to the multiple indicator approach (MIA). Since then, under the MIA, overnight interest rates are gradually emerging as the principal operating target (Mohan, 2005, p. 161), and the central bank considers a variety of economic and financial variables as policy indicators and focuses on their movements to draw future perspectives for policy objectives. The policy indicators consist of interest rates in financial markets, currency, bank credit, fiscal position, trade, capital flows, inflation

---

[1] Operating through repo and reverse repo auctions, the LAF set a corridor for the short-term interest rate, consistent with policy objectives. It enables the RBI to modulate day-to-day liquidity in order to ensure stable conditions in the overnight money market (Mohan, 2005, p. 163). In May 2011, the RBI modified the operating procedures for the LAF (Mohanty, 2011, p. 1436; RBI, 2011, p. 77). The main points were as follows. First, the weighted average overnight call money rate was explicitly recognized as the operating target of monetary policy. Second, the repo rate became the only one independently varying policy rate. Third, a new marginal standing facility (MSF) was instituted under which the scheduled commercial banks could borrow overnight up to 1.0% of their respective net demand and time liabilities at 100 basis points above the repo rate. Fourth, the revised corridor was defined with a fixed width of 200 basis points. The repo rate was placed in the middle of the corridor, with the reverse repo rate 100 basis points below it and the MSF rate 100 basis points above it.

rate, exchange rate, refinancing and transactions in foreign exchange, and output data (Mohan, 2005, p. 162).

Generally, a good policy indicator is defined to provide leading or contemporaneous information on the potential movements in policy objectives, and is normally not treated as an object to be controlled by the central bank (Freedman, 1994, p. 461). Accordingly, in this chapter, we examine the causal relationships of each policy indicator variable with both output and price levels by using the Granger causality test and investigate whether each variable the RBI regards as an indicator actually has a causal relationship with objective variables.

The organization of this chapter is as follows. Section 2.2 reviews the relevant literature. Section 2.3 explains the empirical technique and Section 2.4 presents the definitions and sources of data. In Section 2.5, we present empirical results. Finally, in Section 2.6, we present concluding remarks summarizing the main findings of this study and highlight forthcoming policy issues in India.

2.2 Literature Review

As mentioned above, since the mid-1990s, India's monetary management experienced significant changes. The RBI now aims to achieve its objectives, price stability and economic growth by modulating mainly the short-term interest rate under the MIA. Many studies examine the RBI's conduct of monetary policy mainly through a transmission mechanism.

For example, Singh and Kalirajan (2007) analyzed the effectiveness of the interest rate channel of monetary policy transmission in the post-reform period. Bhattacharyya and Sensarma (2008) examined the impact of monetary policy measures on financial market behavior. Both studies applied the vector autoregression (VAR) model as the empirical method and concluded that during the more recent period, the short-term interest rate played a more important role than the CRR in the monetary transmission mechanism. Meanwhile, Kubo (2009) estimated the impulse response function using a structural VAR model and investigated the monetary transmission mechanism through changes in interest rates, but his conclusion differs in that he found that monetary aggregates' adjustment continued to play a significant role. Besides, Aleem (2010) estimated a series of VAR models to examine the importance of three channels of monetary transmission, that is, the bank lending channel, the asset price channel, and the exchange rate channel, and found that bank lending plays an important role as a transmission channel in India.

Meanwhile, there is limited literature on the monetary policy framework in present-day India. The few relevant prior studies are by Kannan *et al.* (2006) and Samantaraya (2009). Kannan *et al.* (2006) constructed the "monetary conditions index" from a weighted average of the real interest rate, real effective exchange rate, and/or real bank credit growth, and then examined whether they could supplement the existing set of information variables under the MIA. By comparing this index with the actual policy stance, they stated that the index would play the role of a leading indicator of economic activity and inflation rates.

Similarly, Samantaraya (2009) developed the "monetary policy index" by synthesizing qualitative information derived from the RBI governor's statements and quantitative information on M3 growth and the call money rate. Using this index to capture the monetary policy stance, he illustrated that monetary policy instantly influences the interest rate, while it also impacts bank credit, inflation rates, and industrial production, albeit with some lag.

Unlike the previous studies, we investigate whether each variable the RBI regards as indicator variables actually has a causal relationship with objective variables and consider the feasibility of the current monetary policy framework in India.

2.3 Empirical Technique

For empirical analysis, we apply the Granger causality methodology based on the lag-augmented VAR (LA-VAR) model developed by Toda and Yamamoto (1995).[2] In estimating the VAR, it is generally necessary to test whether variables are integrated, cointegrated, or stationary by using the unit root and cointegration tests, since the conventional asymptotic theory is not applicable to hypothesis testing in a level VAR if the variables are integrated or cointegrated (Toda and Yamamoto, 1995, pp. 225–226).

---

[2]Awokuse and Yang (2003) applied the LA-VAR model to examine the causal relationship between commodity prices and macroeconomic variables in the United States from 1975 to 2001. In addition, Hamori (2007) analyzed whether the commodity price index is an information variable for the Bank of Japan by using the LA-VAR model.

However, a unit root test is not powerful enough for hypothesis testing, and the cointegration test is not very reliable for small samples. In order to avoid these potential biases, this study applies the LA-VAR method, which makes it possible to test the coefficient restrictions in a level VAR without considering the properties in the economic time series, such as unit root and cointegration, but which adds *a priori* maximum integration order (d_{max}) to the true lag length (k). This method is summarized in accordance with Toda and Yamamoto (1995) and Hamori (2007) as follows:

First, suppose that the following equation (Equation (1)) generates $\{y_t\}$, the n-dimensional vector constituting the level of the variables in this study:

$$y_t = \alpha_0 + \alpha_1 Time + \beta_1 y_{t-1} + \beta_2 y_{t-2} + \cdots + \beta_k y_{t-k} + e_t,$$

$$t = 1, 2, \ldots, T, \qquad (1)$$

where *Time* is the time trend, k is the true lag length, $\alpha_0, \alpha_1, \beta_1, \beta_2, \ldots, \beta_k$ are the vectors or matrices of coefficients, and e_t is an i.i.d. sequence of n-dimensional random vectors with zero mean and covariance matrix Σ_e.

Next, to test the coefficient restrictions on a subset of parameters in the model formulated as $H_0 : f(\varphi) = 0$, we estimate the VAR model shown in Equation (2) by ordinary least squares:

$$y_t = \hat{\alpha}_0 + \hat{\alpha}_1 Time + \hat{\beta}_1 y_{t-1} + \hat{\beta}_2 y_{t-2} + \cdots + \hat{\beta}_k y_{t-k} + \cdots$$

$$+ \hat{\beta}_p y_{t-p} + \hat{e}_t, \qquad (2)$$

where circumflex indicates the estimates of each variable, and the lag length p equals $k + d_{max} (k \geq d_{max})$. Given that the true values of $\beta_{k+1}, \ldots, \beta_p$ are zero, those parameters are not included in the coefficient restrictions.

Finally, we test the null hypothesis of Granger causality using the Wald test. Asymptotically, the Wald test statistic has a chi-square distribution with the degrees of freedom equal to the excluded number of lagged variables (k).

2.4 Data

The RBI explicitly announced that the policy indicator variables under the MIA consist of a wide range of indicators, such as financial market variables, fiscal balance, trade, and capital flow. Given that quick availability is one of the prerequisites of a policy indicator, however, we focus on monetary aggregates, bank credit (*BC*), stock prices (*SP*), exchange rate (*FX*), and yield spread (*YS*) among the relevant variables. Regarding policy objective variables, we utilize the wholesale price index (*WPI*) and the industrial production index (*IPI*) (seasonally adjusted by X12), since both price stability and economic growth are monetary policy goals in India. We use logarithm values for all variables except for yield spread, which is defined as the difference between the 10-year government bond yield and the call money rate. The exchange rate is the Indian rupee rate against the US dollar.

We obtained *WPI*, *IPI*, stock prices, and exchange rate from the International Monetary Fund (2010). The bank credit, government bond yield, and call rate are from RBI (2009) and monetary aggregates from various issues of the RBI Monthly Bulletin. From 1985 to 1998, the RBI adopted monetary targeting focused on M3 growth as the intermediate target. Even after 1998, the bank emphasizes the development of this broad monetary aggregate as the policy indicator under the MIA. Therefore, with regard to monetary aggregates, we pay special attention to M3, while we also consider M1 and M2 to assess the importance of the information provided by each aggregate.

We use monthly data from April 1998 to June 2009 for the empirical analysis in this study. This corresponds to the period under the current monetary policy framework. In addition, in order to examine whether changes occurred in comparison with the period of previous policy framework, that is, monetary targeting, we considered the sample period from April 1985 to March 1998 as well.

2.5 Empirical Results

We test the causality of an indicator variable on the objective variables by using the trivariate VAR models composed of each policy indicator, and output and price levels. Table 2.1 indicates the Wald test statistic for April 1998 to June 2009. As the MIA was introduced in April 1998, this sample period corresponds to the first eleven years of implementation of the RBI's new monetary policy framework. In this table, we select the true lag length (*k*) from the 12 maximum periods on the basis of the Akaike Information Criterion (AIC) developed by Akaike (1974), while we set the

Table 2.1   Causality During the MIA Period (April 1998 to June 2009)

Explained Variables	Explanatory Variables (k)						
	$M1$ (8)	$M2$ (8)	$M3$ (12)	BC (2)	SP (2)	FX (2)	YS (2)
WPI	12.905	12.950	16.077	1.436	0.575	4.076	8.751**
IPI	15.578**	15.662**	7.462	0.229	23.113***	6.003**	4.976*

Notes: (1) The numbers are the Wald test statistic.
(2) ***, **, and * indicate that the null hypothesis of Granger non-causality is rejected at the 1%, 5%, and 10% significance level, respectively.
(3) k is the lag length selected on the basis of the AIC.
(4) The explained variables are the wholesale price index (*WPI*) and the industrial production index (*IPI*). $M1$, $M2$, and $M3$ are monetary aggregates, *BC* is bank credit, *SP* is stock prices, *FX* is exchange rate, and *YS* is yield spread.

maximum integration order (d_{max}) to 1, since the unit root test shows that the variables are at most integrated of order 1 in all cases except for *YS*, which is stationary in levels.[3]

Table 2.1 presents the following empirical results. First, regarding monetary aggregates, both $M1$ and $M2$ Granger-cause output at the 5% significance level, although $M3$ causes neither output nor price level. Second, similar to $M3$, bank credit lacks a causal relation to any objective variable in the Granger sense. Third, stock prices and the exchange rate cause output level at the 1% and the 5% levels, respectively. Finally, yield spread Granger-causes not only output level at the 10% level, but also price level at the 5% level. In sum, among policy indicators, yield spread could predict the future movements of both output and price levels, while $M1$, $M2$, stock prices, and the exchange rate are useful in predicting only output level.

Table 2.2 provides the Wald test statistic for April 1985 to March 1998, which roughly corresponds to the period in which the RBI adopted monetary targeting. In this table too, we select k on the basis of the AIC, and set d_{max} to 1. Here, we cannot show the result for *YS*, since data on the 10-year

---

[3]These are the results derived by using the Phillips–Perron test (result available upon request). We also conducted the Kwiatkowski–Phillips–Schmidt–Shin test as an alternative unit root test and confirmed that it does not change the results of the Phillips–Perron test except in the case of *FX*, which becomes stationary in levels.

Table 2.2   Causality During the Monetary Targeting Period (April 1985 to March 1998)

Explained Variables	Explanatory Variables (k)					
	$M1$ (3)	$M2$ (3)	$M3$ (2)	BC (2)	SP (3)	FX (2)
WPI	51.408***	50.355***	26.797***	2.990	2.503	2.178
IPI	7.050*	6.910*	1.543	0.612	17.861**	5.211*

Notes: (1) The numbers are the Wald test statistic.
(2) ***, **, and * indicate that the null hypothesis of Granger non-causality is rejected at the 1%, 5%, and 10% significance level, respectively.
(3) k is the lag length selected on the basis of the AIC.
(4) The explained variables are the wholesale price index (*WPI*) and the industrial production index (*IPI*). $M1$, $M2$, and $M3$ are monetary aggregates, *BC* is bank credit, *SP* is stock prices, and *FX* is exchange rate.

government bond yield are not available for this sample period. From this table, we derive the following results. First, regarding monetary aggregates, $M1$ and $M2$ Granger-cause output at the 10% significance level, whereas, $M1$, $M2$, and $M3$ also cause price level at the 1% level. Second, bank credit causes neither output nor price level in the Granger sense. Third, stock prices and the exchange rate cause output level at the 5% and the 10% levels, respectively. In summary, as in Table 2.1, $M1$, $M2$, stock prices, and the exchange rate are found to be useful in predicting output level; however, all monetary aggregates considered also have a causal relation to price level, which contrasts with the results of Table 2.1. Thus, we observe that monetary aggregates have significant causal relationships with the objective variables, perhaps reflecting that the RBI implemented monetary targeting during this sample period. In other words, the results of Tables 2.1 and 2.2 imply a significant change in the relationship between the indicator variables and the objective variables owing to the adoption of the new monetary policy framework in India since 1998.

To check the robustness of our empirical results, we select the true lag length k on the basis of the Schwarz Bayesian Information Criterion (SBIC) developed by Schwarz (1978), instead of the AIC. Despite selecting a different k especially for monetary aggregates, we derive mostly the same results as those in Tables 2.1 and 2.2 (see Tables 2.3 and 2.4). Therefore, in this sense, our findings seem to be robust.

Table 2.3 Causality During the MIA Period (April 1998 to June 2009)

Explained Variables	Explanatory Variables (k)						
	*M*1 (2)	*M*2 (2)	*M*3 (2)	*BC* (2)	*SP* (2)	*FX* (2)	*YS* (2)
WPI	0.369	0.363	3.228	1.436	0.575	4.076	8.751**
IPI	6.067**	6.138**	0.348	0.229	23.113***	6.003**	4.976*

Notes: (1) The numbers are the Wald test statistic.
(2) ***, **, and * indicate that the null hypothesis of Granger non-causality is rejected at the 1%, 5%, and 10% significance level, respectively.
(3) *k* is the lag length selected on the basis of the SBIC.
(4) The explained variables are the wholesale price index (*WPI*) and the industrial production index (*IPI*). *M*1, *M*2, and *M*3 are monetary aggregates, *BC* is bank credit, *SP* is stock prices, *FX* is exchange rate, and *YS* is yield spread.

Table 2.4 Causality During the Monetary Targeting Period (April 1985 to March 1998)

Explained Variables	Explanatory Variables (k)					
	*M*1 (2)	*M*2 (2)	*M*3 (1)	*BC* (1)	*SP* (2)	*FX* (1)
WPI	36.900***	36.505***	20.284***	2.405	1.316	1.989
IPI	6.057**	5.942*	1.680	0.321	14.823**	4.439**

Notes: (1) The numbers are the Wald test statistic.
(2) ***, **, and * indicate that the null hypothesis of Granger non-causality is rejected at the 1%, 5%, and 10% significance level, respectively.
(3) *k* is the lag length selected on the basis of the SBIC.
(4) The explained variables are the wholesale price index (*WPI*) and the industrial production index (*IPI*). *M*1, *M*2, and *M*3 are monetary aggregates, *BC* is bank credit, *SP* is stock prices, and *FX* is exchange rate.

2.6 Concluding Remarks

In 1998, the RBI officially shifted its monetary policy framework from monetary targeting to an MIA. Since then, it appears that the RBI monitors relevant economic and financial variables as policy indicators and utilizes them to draw policy perspectives. It is generally thought that a good indicator or information variable must provide leading or contemporaneous information on future movements in policy objectives, though, unlike the case of an intermediate target, such an indicator or information variable is not under the control of a nation's central bank. Accordingly, in order to examine the effectiveness of the current policy framework in India, this study tested the causal relationships of each policy indicator on the objective variables by employing the LA-VAR model developed by Toda and Yamamoto (1995).

Empirical analysis indicated that under the MIA starting in April 1998, yield spread Granger-causes not only output level but also price level, while M1, M2, stock prices, and the exchange rate are useful in predicting output level. Concomitantly, we conducted causality tests for the period during which monetary targeting was adopted in India, that is, from April 1985 to March 1998. Empirical results showed that monetary aggregates, such as M1, M2, and M3, cause price level in the Granger sense, while M1, M2, stock prices, and the exchange rate are useful in predicting output level. Incidentally, the result for yield spread could not be obtained for the period before 1998, since the required data on the 10-year government bond yield were not available.

In sum, our empirical results indicated that except for bank credit, all indicator variables considered in this study had a causal relationship with either output or price level, suggesting that most preannounced economic and financial variables served as useful policy indicators under the current policy framework in India. Among them, yield spread, in particular, is found to have played an important role, since it contains information for predicting future movements of both output and price levels. Meanwhile, recently, monetary aggregates seem to be playing a weaker role in monetary policy making in India.

Even after the shift from monetary targeting, the RBI still announces the growth rate forecast for M3 and focuses on it as the measure of future price movements in its policy statement. Considering our empirical results, however, it is recommended that the Indian central bank should utilize the information content of M1 and M2, rather than M3, in the process of monetary policy formulation and that it should attach greater importance to newly available yield spread as well as conventional financial variables, including monetary aggregates, stock prices, and the exchange rate.

References

Akaike, H., 1974. A new look at the statistical model identification. *IEEE Transactions on Automatic Control* AC-19, 716–723.

Aleem, A., 2010. Transmission mechanism of monetary policy in India. *Journal of Asian Economics* 21, 186–197.

Awokuse, T.O., Yang, J., 2003. The informational role of commodity prices in formulating monetary policy: A reexamination. *Economics Letters* 79, 219–224.

Bhattacharyya, I., Sensarma, R., 2008. How effective are monetary policy signals in India? *Journal of Policy Modeling* 30, 169–183.

Freedman, C., 1994. The use of indicators and of the monetary conditions index in Canada, in: Balino, T.J.T., Cottarelli, C. (Eds.), *Frameworks for Monetary Stability: Policy Issues and Country Experiences*. International Monetary Fund, Washington, DC, pp. 458–476.

Hamori, S., 2007. The information role of commodity prices in formulating monetary policy: Some evidence from Japan. *Economics Bulletin* 5, 1–7.

International Monetary Fund (IMF), 2010. *International Financial Statistics, April*. IMF, Washington, DC.

Kannan, R., Sanyal, S., Bhoi, B.B., 2006. Monetary conditions index for India. Reserve Bank of India Occasional Papers 27, Reserve Bank of India, Mumbai, 57–86.

Kubo, A., 2009. The effects of monetary policy shock. *Economics Bulletin* 29, 1530–1541.

Mohan, R., 2005. Globalisation, financial markets and the operation of monetary policy in India. *BIS Papers 23*, Bank for International Settlements, Basel, 161–170.

Mohan, R., 2008. Monetary policy transmission in India. *BIS Papers 35*, Bank for International Settlements, Basel, 259–307.

Mohanty, D., 2011. How does the Reserve Bank of India conduct its monetary policy? *RBI Monthly Bulletin September*, Reserve Bank of India, Mumbai, 1431–1439.

Reddy, Y.V., 2005. Monetary policy: An outline. *RBI Monthly Bulletin March*, Reserve Bank of India, Mumbai, 219–223.

Reserve Bank of India (RBI), 2009. *Handbook of Statistics on Indian Economy 2008–09*. RBI, Mumbai.

Reserve Bank of India (RBI), 2011. *Annual Report 2010–11*. RBI, Mumbai.

Reserve Bank of India (RBI), various issues. *RBI Monthly Bulletin*. RBI, Mumbai.

Samantaraya, A., 2009. An index to assess the stance of monetary policy in India in the post-reform period. *Economic and Political Weekly* 44, 46–50.

Schwarz, G., 1978. Estimating the dimension of a model. *The Annals of Statistics* 6, 461–464.

Singh, K., Kalirajan, K., 2007. Monetary transmission in post-reform India: An evaluation. *Journal of the Asia Pacific Economy* 12, 158–187.

Toda, H.Y., Yamamoto, T., 1995. Statistical inference in vector autoregressions with possibly integrated processes. *Journal of Econometrics* 66, 225–250.

Chapter 3

Is India Ready to Adopt a Policy Framework Targeting Inflation?

3.1 Introduction

Since the end of the 1990s, the Reserve Bank of India (RBI) has aimed to achieve its objectives, that is, price stability and economic growth, by mainly modulating the short-term interest rate under the multiple indicator approach wherein movements not only in money supply but also in a host of other macroeconomic variables have been tracked for policy responses.

Recently, regarding monetary policy procedure in India, some official committee submitted a formal report to the Indian government. For instance, GOI (2007) states that "the monetary authority needs to consider focusing exclusively on the single task of managing a key short-term 'base rate' to maintain price stability (e.g., inflation being kept within a range of 3–4%), consistent with supporting a high growth rate (8–10%)." Similarly, GOI (2009) recommends that "the RBI should formally have a single objective, to stay close to a low inflation number, or within a range, in the medium term, and move steadily to a single instrument, the short-term interest rate (repo and reverse repo), to achieve it."

As epitomized by these proposals, there are some arguments that the RBI should focus more on price stability than on economic activity, and finally should adopt inflation targeting, although, most relevant studies have a negative view on it (Singh, 2006; Chakraborty, 2008; Jha, 2008). In this chapter, we estimate India's monetary policy reaction function utilizing the Taylor (1993) rule, examine how the short-term interest rate has an effect on inflation rate, and consider whether India is ready to adopt the inflation-targeting type of policy framework or not.

We begin by reviewing the relevant literature and discussing the contributions of this study. Section 3.3 presents our models, and Section 3.4 provides the definitions, sources, and properties of the data. In Section 3.5, we give the empirical results of the study. This chapter ends with a summary of our main findings and offers some policy implications.

3.2   Literature Review

In his seminal work, Taylor (1993) formulated a policy rule by which the Federal Reserve adjusts the policy rate in response to lagged inflation and the real gross domestic product gap, and he showed that this rule accurately described the actual policy performance from 1987 through 1992. Since then, a number of studies, such as Clarida *et al.* (1998, 2000), Peersman and Smets (1999), Chadha *et al.* (2004), and Fendel and Frenkel (2006), have applied and modified this policy rule to examine the behaviors of central banks in industrialized countries and regions. In contrast, there have been few empirical analyses on monetary policy rules for developing countries. In India's context, the examples are Mohanty and Klau (2004) and Virmani (2004).

Following Taylor (2001), Mohanty and Klau (2004) extended the Taylor rule to include changes in the real effective exchange rate (REER) and examined how the central bank changes the policy rate in response to inflation, output gap, and exchange rate. They used quarterly data from 1995 to 2002 in 13 emerging economies, including India. The empirical results of the ordinary least squares (OLS) and generalized method of moments (GMM) estimations for India showed that all explanatory variables are significant with the expected signs, and that the interest rate responds to exchange rate volatility to a greater extent than inflation and the output gap.

Also, Virmani (2004) estimated India's monetary policy reaction function by using the Taylor rule as well as the McCallum (1988) rule augmented with change in the REER. The sample period spanned from the third quarter of 1992 to the fourth quarter of 2001. From the OLS and GMM estimations, it was found that the backward-looking Taylor rule captures the evolution of the short-term interest rate reasonably well and that the backward-looking McCallum rule also performs quite well.

As discussed above, the literature (except for Inoue and Hamori, 2012) has used the standard OLS and/or GMM estimation methods, with the exchange rate as the important variable, especially for monetary policy rules in emerging market economies. In line with the literature, our examination estimates two different kinds of rules, that is, the Taylor rule and its augmented model with the exchange rate as the objective variable. We refer to the former as the simple Taylor rule, and the latter, the open economy Taylor rule. Following Inoue and Hamori (2012), we take into consideration the nonstationarity of each variable and apply both the dynamic OLS (DOLS) (Saikkonen, 1992; Stock and Watson, 1993) and fully modified OLS (FMOLS; Phillips and Hansen, 1990) methods instead of standard OLS and/or GMM estimations, and shed light on the characteristics of India's monetary policy reaction function by examining the sign conditions and the statistical significance of variable coefficients.

3.3 Models

The simple Taylor rule is shown as follows:

Model 1: $$r_t = a_0 + a_1 \pi_t + a_2 y_t, \quad a_1 > 0, a_2 > 0, \tag{1}$$

where r_t is the nominal interest rate at time t, π_t is the inflation rate at time t, and y_t is the output gap at time t. According to the rule, both a_1 and a_2 should be positive. That is, the rule indicates a relatively high interest rate when inflation is above its target or when the output is above its potential level, and a relatively low interest rate when inflation is below its target or when the output is below its potential level.

Following Taylor (2001) and Chadha *et al.* (2004), we empirically analyze the role of the exchange rate as the next step. Here, the simple Taylor rule is extended to include the exchange rate as an additional explanatory variable as follows:

Model 2: $$r_t = b_0 + b_1 \pi_t + b_2 y_t + b_3 e_t, \quad b_1 > 0, b_2 > 0, b_3 < 0. \tag{2}$$

Model 3: $$r_t = c_0 + c_1 \pi_t + c_2 y_t + c_3 \ln(e_t), \quad c_1 > 0, c_2 > 0, c_3 < 0. \tag{3}$$

In this augmented rule, e_t represents the REER at time t, and its coefficient is expected to have a negative sign. Equation (2) uses the exchange rate itself, while Equation (3) uses the log of exchange rate. These indicate a relatively high interest rate when the real exchange rate depreciates and a relatively low interest rate when the real exchange rate appreciates.

3.4　Data

We use monthly data from April 1998 to March 2009. The data for the industrial production index (IPI) (seasonally adjusted by X12) and the producer price index were sourced from the International Monetary Fund (2013). The IPI is a proxy for the output. We use the call rate as the interest rate. The call rates were sourced from RBI (2008, 2011, 2013), whereas the REER was obtained from RBI (2013).

We calculate the output gap in the following way. First, we regress the output on a constant and a time trend.

$$\ln(Y_t) = \alpha + \beta \times time + u_t, \tag{4}$$

where Y_t is the output at time t, *time* is the time trend, and u_t is the error term with mean 0 and finite variance. The potential output is described as the predicted value of Equation (4).

$$\ln(Y_t^*) = \hat{\alpha} + \hat{\beta} \times time, \tag{5}$$

where Y_t^* is the potential output, and $\hat{\alpha}$ and $\hat{\beta}$ are estimates of α and β. We then calculate the output gap as the deviation of output from its potential level as follows:

$$y_t = 100 \times (\ln(Y_t) - \ln(Y_t^*))$$
$$= 100 \times \ln\left(1 + \frac{Y_t - Y_t^*}{Y_t^*}\right) \cong 100 \times \frac{Y_t - Y_t^*}{Y_t^*}, \tag{6}$$

where y_t is the output gap at time t. Figure 3.1 indicates the movement of output gap.

We also calculate the inflation rate as the log difference of the price level from the previous year as follows.

$$\pi_t = 100 \times (\ln(p_t) - \ln(p_{t-12}))$$
$$= 100 \times \ln\left(1 + \frac{p_t - p_{t-12}}{p_{t-12}}\right) \cong 100 \times \frac{p_t - p_{t-12}}{p_{t-12}}, \tag{7}$$

where p_t is the price level at time t.

Figure 3.1   Output Gap

As a preliminary analysis, we conduct the augmented Dickey–Fuller tests for the output gap, interest rates, inflation rates, and the REER (Dickey and Fuller, 1979). As a result, the level of each variable is found to have a unit root, whereas the opposite is true for the first difference of each variable. Thus, we can say that each variable is a nonstationary variable with a unit root.

3.5 Empirical Techniques

When we estimate the cointegrating vector, we cannot use OLS due to the problem of endogeneity for regressors. Phillips and Hansen (1990) proposed a single-equation method based on OLS with semi-parametric correction for serial correlation and endogeneity, which is FMOLS. Let the dependent variable be denoted by y_t and the vector of regressors, by x_t, where x_t is an $m \times 1$ vector and $t = 1, 2, \ldots, T$. The behavior of y_t and x_t is assumed to satisfy

$$y_t = x_t'\beta + d_t'\alpha + u_{1t}, \tag{8}$$

$$x_t = x_{t-1} + u_{2t}, \tag{9}$$

where d_t is a vector of deterministic trend regressors. Let $u_t = (u_{1t}, u_{2t}')'$ be a joint innovation process; then, the one-sided long-run covariance matrix

Λ and long-run covariance matrix Ω can be expressed as follows:

$$\Lambda = \sum_{i=0}^{\infty} E(u_t u_{t-i}') = \begin{bmatrix} \lambda_{11} & \lambda_{12} \\ \lambda_{21} & \Lambda_{22} \end{bmatrix}, \tag{10}$$

$$\Omega = \sum_{i=-\infty}^{\infty} E(u_t u_{t-i}') = \begin{bmatrix} \omega_{11} & \omega_{12} \\ \omega_{21} & \Omega_{22} \end{bmatrix}. \tag{11}$$

Let $y_t^+ = y_t - \hat{\omega}_{12}\hat{\Omega}_{22}^{-1}\Delta x_t$ and $\hat{\lambda}_{12}^+ = \hat{\lambda}_{12} - \hat{\omega}_{12}\hat{\Omega}_{22}^{-1}\hat{\Lambda}_{22}$, where $\hat{\lambda}_{12}, \hat{\omega}_{12}, \hat{\Omega}_{22}^{-1}$ and $\hat{\Lambda}_{22}$ are consistent estimates of the respective parameters. The FMOLS estimator is given by

$$\begin{bmatrix} \hat{\beta} \\ \hat{\alpha} \end{bmatrix} = \left(\sum_{t=1}^{T} z_t z_t' \right)^{-1} \left(\sum_{t=1}^{T} z_t y_t^+ - T \begin{bmatrix} \hat{\lambda}_{12}^{+\prime} \\ 0 \end{bmatrix} \right), \tag{12}$$

where $z_t = (x_t', d_t')'$.

Saikkonen (1992) and Stock and Watson (1993) proposed DOLS as a simple efficient estimator. The DOLS specification simply adds leads and lags of the first difference of stochastic regressors to the standard cointegrating regression:

$$y_t = x_t'\beta + d_t'\alpha + \sum_{i=-K}^{K} \Delta x_{t+i}'\gamma + v_t. \tag{13}$$

Obtained from Equation (13), the DOLS estimator, $(\hat{\beta}', \hat{\alpha}')'$, has the same asymptotic distribution as those obtained from FMOLS.

3.6 Empirical Results

3.6.1 Simple Taylor rule

First, we conduct Johansen-type cointegration tests for the policy reaction function (Johansen and Juselius, 1990; Johansen, 1991). This test is of two types: the trace test and the maximum eigenvalue test. Table 3.1 shows the results of the cointegration tests. As is evident from Table 3.1, the null hypothesis of no cointegrating relation is rejected at the 5% significance

Table 3.1   Cointegration Tests (Simple Taylor Rule)

Null Hypothesis	Trace Test	Maximum Eigenvalue Test
System (r_t, π_t, y_t)		
$r = 0$	44.077	33.240
	(0.001)	(0.001)

Notes: (1) Numbers in parentheses are *p*-values.
(2) r is the hypothesized number of cointegrating equations.

Table 3.2   Cointegrating Regression (Simple Taylor Rule)

Variable	Coefficient	SE	*t*-Statistic	*p*-value	$\bar{R}^2$
Model 1: $r_t = a_0 + a_1\pi_t + a_2 y_t$					
DOLS					
Constant	8.757	1.231	7.115	0.000	0.282
π_t	−0.300	0.231	−1.297	0.197	
y_t	0.419	0.114	3.667	0.000	
FMOLS					
Constant	6.906	0.757	9.126	0.000	0.243
π_t	0.058	0.131	0.440	0.660	
y_t	0.345	0.087	3.945	0.000	

Notes: (1) SE is the Newey–West heteroskedasticity and autocorrelation consistent (HAC) Standard Error.
(2) π is the inflation rate, and y is the output gap.

level.[1] Thus, it is likely that there is a cointegrating relationship among interest rates, inflation rates, and the output gap.

Since the existence of the cointegrating relation is supported, we estimate the Taylor rule. Table 3.2 shows the estimation results based on DOLS and FMOLS. The output coefficient is estimated to be positive (0.419 for DOLS and 0.345 for FMOLS) and statistically significant at the 1% level. On the other hand, the inflation rate coefficient is estimated to be −0.300 for DOLS and 0.058 for FMOLS but is not statistically significant.[2]

---

[1]The lag order is set to be 6.
[2]The order of lead and lag is set to be 4 for DOLS.

Table 3.3 Cointegration Tests (Open Economy Taylor Rule)

Null Hypothesis	Trace Test	Maximum Eigenvalue Test
System (r_t, π_t, y_t, e_t)		
$r = 0$	64.133	35.687
	(0.001)	(0.004)
System $(r_t, \pi_t, y_t, \ln(e_t))$		
$r = 0$	66.555	38.478
	(0.000)	(0.001)

Notes: (1) Numbers in parentheses are *p*-values.
(2) r is the hypothesized number of cointegrating equations.

3.6.2 Open economy Taylor rule

Next, we analyze India's monetary policy reaction function by applying the Taylor rule augmented with the exchange rate. Prior to estimation, we conduct Johansen-type cointegration tests for the short-term interest rate, inflation rate, output gap, and exchange rate for Model 2. We also conduct Johansen-type cointegration tests for the short-term interest rate, inflation rate, output gap, and the log of exchange rate for Model 3. Table 3.3 shows the results of the cointegration tests. The null hypothesis of no cointegrating relation is rejected in all cases at the 1% level. Thus, there is a cointegrating relationship among variables for both systems.

Since the existence of the cointegrating relation is supported, we estimate the extended Taylor rule using DOLS and FMOLS.[3] Table 3.4 shows the estimation results for Model 2. The output coefficient is estimated to be positive (0.430 for DOLS and 0.381 for FMOLS) and statistically significant at the 1% level. The inflation rate coefficient is estimated to be −0.457 for DOLS and 0.023 for FMOLS but is not statistically significant. These results are consistent with those obtained in Table 3.2. It is notable that the estimate of the coefficient of the REER is negative (−0.191 for DOLS and −0.166 for FMOLS) and statistically significant at the 5% level.

---

[3]The order of lead and lag is set to be 6 for DOLS.

Table 3.4   Cointegrating Regression (Open Economy Taylor Rule)

Variable	Coefficient	SE	t-Statistic	p-value	$\bar{R}^2$
Model 2: $r_t = b_0 + b_1\pi_t + b_2 y_t + b_3 e_t$					
DOLS					
Constant	28.632	7.388	3.876	0.000	0.486
π_t	−0.457	0.270	−1.696	0.093	
y_t	0.430	0.079	5.472	0.000	
e_t	−0.191	0.078	−2.451	0.016	
FMOLS					
Constant	23.632	5.713	4.137	0.000	0.337
π_t	0.023	0.116	0.196	0.845	
y_t	0.381	0.078	4.895	0.000	
e_t	−0.166	0.056	−2.954	0.004	
Model 3: $r_t = c_0 + c_1\pi_t + c_2 y_t + c_3 \ln(e_t)$					
DOLS					
Constant	123.738	34.537	3.583	0.001	0.532
π_t	−0.427	0.250	−1.705	0.092	
y_t	0.449	0.074	6.057	0.000	
$\ln(e_t)$	−24.825	7.602	−3.266	0.002	
FMOLS					
Constant	79.511	26.214	3.033	0.003	0.339
π_t	0.026	0.117	0.222	0.825	
y_t	0.375	0.079	4.756	0.000	
$\ln(e_t)$	−15.738	5.677	−2.772	0.006	

Notes: (1) SE is the Newey–West HAC Standard Error.
(2) π is the inflation rate, y is the output gap, and e is the REER.

Table 3.4 also shows the estimation results for Model 3. The output coefficient is estimated to be positive (0.449 for DOLS and 0.375 for FMOLS) and statistically significant at the 1% level. The inflation rate coefficient is estimated to be −0.427 for DOLS and 0.026 for FMOLS but is not statistically significant. It is notable that the estimate of the coefficient of the REER is negative (−24.825 for DOLS and −15.738 for FMOLS) and statistically significant at the 1% level. The results obtained in Table 3.4 for Model 3 are consistent with those obtained for Model 2.

3.7 Concluding Remarks

In this chapter, we empirically analyzed India's monetary policy reaction function by applying the simple Taylor rule and its open-economy model. The analysis employed both the FMOLS and DOLS methods, and used monthly data from the period of April 1998 to March 2009. When the simple Taylor rule was estimated for India, the output gap coefficient was statistically significant, and its sign condition was found to be consistent with theoretical rationale. However, the same was not true of the inflation coefficient, i.e., the inflation coefficient was statistically insignificant. Next, when the open economy Taylor rule was estimated, the coefficients of output gap and exchange rate had statistical significance with the expected signs, whereas the results of inflation remained the same as before.

Conceptually, inflation targeting is defined as the policy framework which seeks to stabilize prices by adjusting interest rate based on inflation forecasts. Although the chosen monetary policy rule is simple, our empirical results suggest that India's monetary policy could respond appropriately to internal supply-demand gaps and external competitiveness, but not to changes in price level. In other words, the short-term interest rate is not yet an effective instrument to control the inflation rate, suggesting that India has failed to meet one of the key preconditions for inflation targeting. Accordingly, based on empirical results, it has been concluded that the RBI is not ready to focus more on the inflation rate, let alone adopt an inflation-targeting-type policy framework.

References

Chadha, J.S., Sarno, L., Valente, G., 2004. Monetary policy rules, asset prices, and exchange rates. IMF Staff Papers 51, International Monetary Fund, Washington, DC, 529–552.

Chakraborty, L., 2008. Analysing the Raghuram Rajan Committee report on financial sector reforms. *Economic and Political Weekly* 143, 11–14.

Clarida, R., Gali, J., Gertler, M., 1998. Monetary policy rule in practice: Some international evidence. NBER Working Paper 6254, The National Bureau of Economic Research, Cambridge, MA.

Clarida, R., Gali, J., Gertler, M., 2000. Monetary policy rules and macroeconomic stability: Evidence and some theory. *The Quarterly Journal of Economics* 115, 147–180.

Dickey, D.A., Fuller, W.A., 1979. Distribution of the estimators for autoregressive time series with a unit root. *Journal of the American Statistical Association* 74, 427–431.

Fendel, R.M., Frenkel, M.R., 2006. Five years of single European monetary policy in practice: Is the ECB rule-based? *Contemporary Economic Policy* 24, 106–115.

Government of India (GOI), 2007. *Report of the High Powered Expert Committee on Making Mumbai an International Financial Centre.* GOI, New Delhi.

Government of India (GOI), 2009. *A Hundred Small Steps: Report of the Committee on Financial Sector Reforms.* GOI, New Delhi.

Inoue, T., Hamori, S., 2012. An empirical analysis of the monetary policy reaction function in India. *The Indian Economic Journal* 60, 126–133.

International Monetary Fund (IMF), 2013. *International Financial Statistics, November.* IMF, Washington, DC.

Jha, R., 2008. Inflation targeting in India: Issues and prospects. *International Review of Applied Economics* 22, 259–270.

Johansen, S., 1991. Estimation and hypothesis testing of cointegration vectors in Gaussian vector autoregressive models. *Econometrica* 59, 1551–1580.

Johansen, S., Juselius, K., 1990. Maximum likelihood estimation and inference on cointegration — With applications to the demand for money. *Oxford Bulletin of Economics and Statistics* 52, 169–210.

McCallum, B.T., 1988. Robustness properties of a rule for monetary policy. *Carnegie-Rochester Series on Public Policy* 29, 173–203.

Mohanty, M.S., Klau, M., 2004. Monetary policy rules in emerging market economies: Issues and evidence. BIS Working Paper 149, Bank for International Settlements, Basel.

Peersman, G., Smets, F., 1999. The Taylor rule: A useful monetary policy benchmark for the euro area. *International Finance* 2, 85–116.

Phillips, P.C.B., Hansen, B.E., 1990. Statistical inference in instrumental variables regression with I(1) processes. *Review of Economic Studies* 57, 99–125.

Reserve Bank of India (RBI), 2008. *Handbook of Statistics on Indian Economy 2007–08.* RBI, Mumbai.

Reserve Bank of India (RBI), 2011. *Handbook of Statistics on Indian Economy 2010–11.* RBI, Mumbai.

Reserve Bank of India (RBI), 2013. *Handbook of Statistics on Indian Economy 2012–13.* RBI, Mumbai.

Saikkonen, P., 1992. Estimation and testing of cointegrated systems by an autoregressive approximation. *Econometric Theory* 8, 1–27.

Singh, K., 2006. Inflation targeting: International experience and prospects for India. *Economic and Political Weekly* 41, 2958–2961.

Stock, J.H., Watson, M.W., 1993. A simple estimator of cointegrating vectors in higher order integrated systems. *Econometrica* 61, 783–820.

Taylor, J.B., 1993. Discretion versus policy rules in practice. *Carnegie-Rochester Conference Series on Public Policy* 39, 195–214.

Taylor, J.B., 2001. The role of the exchange rate in monetary-policy rules. *American Economic Review* 91, 263–267.

Virmani, V., 2004. Operationalising Taylor-type rules for the Indian economy: Issues and some results (1992Q3–2001Q4). IIMA Working Papers 2004-07-04, Indian Institute of Management, Ahmedabad.

Part 2

Financial Markets in India

Chapter 4

Causal Relationships in Mean and Variance between Stock Returns and Foreign Institutional Investment in India

4.1 Introduction

In September 1992, the Government of India threw open the domestic stock market to foreign institutional investors. Since then, foreign institutional investment (FII) has steadily grown as the primary source of portfolio investment in India, playing a more important role than domestic investment.[1] Reflecting high economic growth, favorable corporate performance, and international liquidity, this tendency has become more significant since mid-2003. Since around May 2003, purchases by foreign institutional investors have outstripped sales, especially in the case of Indian equities (see Figure 4.1).

This surge of FII inflows is said to have affected the Indian economy, especially the secondary stock market, given the dominant role of equity in FII inflows and the low level of floating stocks. In fact, the Bombay Stock Exchange (BSE) SENSEX 30, the leading index in the principal market, has shown a significant upward movement since net FII flows began to

---

[1]Between January 2000 and March 2008, the average and standard deviation of net investments by foreign institutional investors were Rs. 2,312 crore and Rs. 4,839 crore, respectively. The corresponding figures for domestic mutual funds were Rs. 333 crore and Rs. 1,626 crore, respectively. This indicates that FII has been larger and more volatile than domestic major investment.

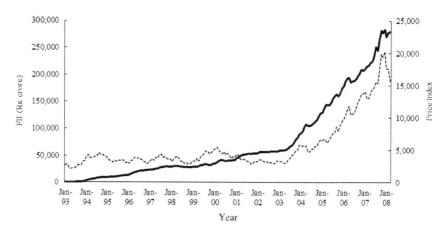

Figure 4.1   Cumulative Net FII and Stock Price Index

Source: Datastream and RBI (2008b).
Note: The bold line represents the cumulative net FII, and the dotted line, the BSE SENSEX 30 stock price index.

increase, that is, since around mid-2003.[2] A similar trend is observed even when data are expressed in real terms (see Figure 4.2).

There are several theoretical explanations for this co-movement. One is that foreign institutional investors may adjust their portfolio allocations depending on stock price movements. In this case, the surge in FII stems from the increase in stock returns. The increase in portfolio inflows following the rise in stock returns is generally called positive feedback trading, while the increase in portfolio inflows after stock returns decline is referred to as negative feedback trading. Conversely, FII volume may be large enough to affect stock prices in the host country. In this case, a stock price boom can be attributed to the amount of trading by foreign institutional investors.

Previous studies using data for India before 2003 have found that while stock returns have an impact on the movement of FII, vice versa is untrue, although the central bank's publications and Indian business newspapers frequently point out that the behavior of foreign investors influences the movement of share prices. Using data since 2003, this research will investigate the causal relationship between FII flows and stock returns in

---

[2]In general, net private capital inflows to emerging market economies have increased sharply since 2002 (Committee on the Global Financial System, 2009).

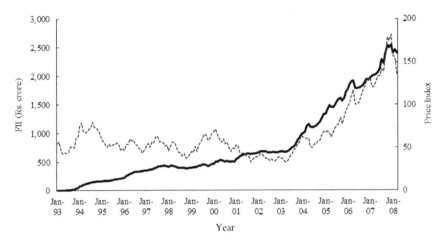

Figure 4.2   Cumulative Net FII and Stock Price Index in Real Terms

Source: Datastream, IMF (2009), and RBI (2008b).
Notes: (1) The bold line represents the cumulative net FII, and the dotted line, the BSE SENSEX 30 stock price index.
(2) The figures are deflated by the wholesale price index.

India. In this examination, we will apply the cross-correlation function (CCF) approach developed by Cheung and Ng (1996) to find the causalities in both the mean and the variance between the said variables. We will also conduct a Granger causality test based on the lag-augmented vector autoregression (LA-VAR) developed by Toda and Yamamoto (1995) to confirm the robustness of the empirical results.

Section 4.2 reviews the related literature and explains the nature of this study. Section 4.3 gives a brief explanation of the CCF approach, while Section 4.4 provides the definitions, sources, and properties of the data. Section 4.5 conducts the Granger causality test as a preliminary test to ascertain whether the stock price index affects net FII flows and/or vice versa, and followed by the CCF approach to test the causalities in the mean and variance between stock returns and net FII flows. Finally, Section 4.6 summarizes the main findings of this work and draw some policy implications.

4.2 Literature Review

International portfolio investment in developing countries has been volatile during the last two decades. Except for 1995, from 1992–1997, net private portfolio inflows into developing countries fluctuated between USD 50 billion and USD 90 billion. Subsequently, however, reflecting the Asian and Russian financial crises, they turned negative and recorded net outflows from 1999 to 2001. In 2002, portfolio investments again showed net inflows, but since then, they have fluctuated between net inflows and net outflows within the range of USD 5 billion to USD 15 billion.

Portfolio investment in India also followed the general trend in developing countries during the 1990s. Net inflows expanded from USD 4 million (Rs. 9 crore) in 1991 to USD 242 million (Rs. 627 crore) in 1992 and to USD 3,647 million (Rs. 11,121 crore) in 1993.[3] After remaining stable for the next three years, they turned negative and recorded net outflows in 1998. Unlike other developing countries, however, since 2003, India has continued to attract large amounts of portfolio investments. Net inflows increased to USD 11,356 million (Rs. 52,900 crore) in 2003 and reached USD 29,096 million (Rs. 120,308 crore) in 2007. As a result, India has become one of the largest recipients of portfolio inflows among emerging market economies (RBI, 2008a, p. 154).

Along with the experience of the financial crisis in emerging markets in the late 1990s, previous literature also indicates that portfolio investment has the potential to become volatile more often than direct investment, and therefore, it can destabilize asset markets and real economic activity in a host economy. In India, portfolio investment has mainly been driven by FII in equity, which has increased, on a cumulative basis, to an amount comparable to foreign direct investment in India. Considering that the Indian capital market is still thin with a relatively low turnover and therefore, is likely to be influenced by the trading behavior of foreign investors, previous research has examined the statistical relationships between FII equity flows and stock returns and/or other related factors. For example, Chakrabarti (2001) conducted an empirical study of the relationship between FII flows and stock returns in India by applying a pairwise Granger causality test. Using daily data from January 1, 1999 to December 31, 1999, he found that FII flows are more likely to be the effect, rather than the cause, of market returns, although the results based on monthly data from July 1993 to December 1999 suggested that this relationship is statistically insignificant at the

---

[3]A crore is equal to 10 million (10,000,000).

conventional level. Furthermore, using the same monthly data, Chakrabarti (2001) regressed FII flows on stock returns and other relevant variables identified in the literature and showed that market returns became the sole driving force behind FII flows into India following the Asian financial crisis.

Mukherjee *et al.* (2002) supplemented and developed the empirical research by Chakrabarti (2001) using extended daily data for the period of January 1, 1999 to May 31, 2002. They first ran a pairwise Granger causality test and confirmed the results of Chakrabarti (2001), namely that there was a uni-directional causality from Indian stock returns to FII flows during their sample period. Mukherjee *et al.* (2002) then estimated the impacts of lagged stock returns and other relevant variables, such as industrial production, call money rate, and exchange rate, on FII flows and found that market returns are perhaps the single most important factor determining FII flows.

Thereafter, Gordon and Gupta (2003) examined the determinants of FII equity flows into India in a multivariate regression model using monthly data from March 1993 to October 2001. While framing the empirical analysis, they separated the determinants into domestic macroeconomic, global, and regional factors, and they investigated the statistical significance of each factor. Their empirical results showed that a combination of these factors is important in the regressions and lagged stock returns individually exert the greatest influence on FII flows, followed by emerging market returns, and credit rating downgrades. Lagged stock returns were also found to be negatively associated with FII flows, suggesting that foreign institutional investors are negative feedback traders.

Finally, Griffin *et al.* (2002) analyzed the relationships between equity flows into a country and the stock returns of that country or the stock returns in the rest of the world for India and eight other emerging countries. By applying a bivariate structural VAR and using daily data from December 31, 1998 to February 23, 2001, Griffin *et al.* (2002) obtained empirical results that greatly differed from those of related studies. While they rejected the null hypothesis that net foreign flows do not cause Indian stock returns in the Granger sense, they could not reject the null hypothesis that past stock returns do not cause net foreign flows in the Granger sense. In addition, they pointed out that stock returns in North America have a statistically significant effect on equity flows toward Asian countries including India.

Except for Griffin *et al.* (2002), the literature reviewed here indicates that stock returns can explain FII flows into India to a greater extent than other factors. These studies, however, examined the period before 2003. Given the structural change in stock prices and net FII flows since mid-2003, it would be worthwhile to re-investigate this relationship using more recent data. Therefore, we will make an empirical examination of the causal relationship between stock returns and FII flows using daily data for the period starting January 1, 1999 and ending March 31, 2008. Unlike the reviewed literature, this work relies primarily on the CCF approach for its estimations.

4.3 Empirical Technique

The CCF approach was developed by Cheung and Ng (1996) to examine the causalities in the mean and variance between variables. This approach is based on the residual cross-correlation function and consists of a two-stage procedure (Cheung and Ng, 1996, p. 34). The first stage involves the estimation of univariate time series models that allow for time variation in both the conditional means and the conditional variances. In the second stage, the resulting series of residuals and squared residuals, standardized by conditional variance, are constructed. The CCF of the standardized residuals is used to test the null hypothesis of no causality in mean, whereas the CCF of the squared-standardized residuals is used to test the null hypothesis of no causality in variance. The approach used in this work is also in accordance with Hong (2001) and Hamori (2003) and is summarized below.

Suppose that there are two stationary time series, X_t and Y_t, with three information sets, which are defined as $I_{1t} = \{X_{t-j}; j \geq 0\}$, $I_{2t} = \{Y_{t-j}; j \geq 0\}$, and $I_t = \{X_{t-j}, Y_{t-j}; j \geq 0\}$. Y_t is said to cause X_t in mean if

$$E\{X_t|I_{1t-1}\} \neq E\{X_t|I_{t-1}\}. \tag{1}$$

Similarly, X_t is said to cause Y_t in mean if

$$E\{Y_t|I_{2t-1}\} \neq E\{Y_t|I_{t-1}\}. \tag{2}$$

We encounter feedback in mean if Y_t causes X_t in mean, and vice versa.

Y_t, on the other hand, is said to cause X_t in variance if

$$E\{(X_t - \mu_{x,t})^2 | I_{1t-1}\} \neq E\{(X_t - \mu_{x,t})^2 | I_{t-1}\}, \tag{3}$$

where $\mu_{x,t}$ is the mean of X_t conditioned on I_{1t-1}. Similarly, X_t causes Y_t in variance if

$$E\{(Y_t - \mu_{y,t})^2 | I_{2t-1}\} \neq E\{(Y_t - \mu_{y,t})^2 | I_{t-1}\}, \tag{4}$$

where $\mu_{y,t}$ is the mean of Y_t conditioned on I_{2t-1}. We encounter feedback in variance if X_t causes Y_t in variance, and vice versa.

The concept defined in Equations 1–4 is too general to be tested empirically. Hence, we need to add another structure to the general causality concept so as to make it practically applicable. Suppose X_t and Y_t can be written as

$$X_t = \mu_{x,t} + h_{x,t}^{0.5} \varepsilon_t, \tag{5}$$

$$Y_t = \mu_{y,t} + h_{y,t}^{0.5} \xi_t, \tag{6}$$

where $\{\varepsilon_t\}$ and $\{\xi_t\}$ are two independent white noise processes with zero mean and unit variance, respectively, and $h_{x,t}$ and $h_{y,t}$ are the conditional variances of X_t and Y_t, respectively. For the causality-in-mean test, we can use the following standardized innovation:

$$\varepsilon_t = (X_t - \mu_{x,t}) h_{x,t}^{-0.5}, \tag{7}$$

$$\xi_t = (Y_t - \mu_{y,t}) h_{y,t}^{-0.5}. \tag{8}$$

As both $\{\varepsilon_t\}$ and $\{\xi_t\}$ are unobservable, we must use their estimates, $\hat{\varepsilon}_t$ and $\hat{\xi}_t$, to test the hypothesis of no causality in mean.

Next, we compute the sample cross-correlation coefficient at lag i, $\hat{r}_{\varepsilon\xi}(i)$ from the consistent estimates of the conditional mean and variance of X_t and Y_t. This leaves us with

$$\hat{r}_{\varepsilon\xi}(i) = C_{\varepsilon\xi}(i)(C_{\varepsilon\varepsilon}(0) C_{\xi\xi}(0))^{-0.5}, \tag{9}$$

where $C_{\varepsilon\xi}(i)$ is ith lag sample cross-covariance, given by

$$C_{\varepsilon\xi}(i) = T^{-1} \sum (\hat{\varepsilon}_t - \bar{\hat{\varepsilon}})(\hat{\xi}_{t-i} - \bar{\hat{\xi}}), \quad i = 0, \pm 1, \pm 2, \ldots, \tag{10}$$

and, similarly, where $C_{\varepsilon\varepsilon}(0)$ and $C_{\xi\xi}(0)$ are defined as the sample variance of ε_t and ξ_t, respectively.

Causality in mean of X_t and Y_t can be tested by examining $\hat{r}_{\varepsilon\xi}(i)$, the univariate standardized residual CCF. Under the condition of regularity, it holds that

$$\begin{pmatrix} \sqrt{T}\hat{r}_{\varepsilon\xi}(i) \\ \sqrt{T}\hat{r}_{\varepsilon\xi}(i') \end{pmatrix} \xrightarrow{L} AN\left(\begin{bmatrix} 0 \\ 1 \end{bmatrix}, \begin{bmatrix} 1 & 0 \\ 0 & 1 \end{bmatrix}\right), \quad i \neq i', \tag{11}$$

where $\xrightarrow{L}$ shows the convergence in the distribution.

This test statistic can be used to test the null hypothesis of no causality in mean. To test for a causal relationship at a specified lag i, we compare $\hat{r}_{\varepsilon\xi}(i)$ with the standard normal distribution. If the test statistic is larger than the critical value of the normal distribution, we reject the null hypothesis.

For the causality-in-variance test, let U_t and V_t be the squares of the standardized innovations, given by

$$U_t = (X_t - \mu_{x,t})^2 h_{x,t}^{-1} = \varepsilon_t^2, \tag{12}$$

$$V_t = (Y_t - \mu_{y,t})^2 h_{y,t}^{-1} = \xi_t^2. \tag{13}$$

As both U_t and V_t are unobservable, we must use their estimates, $\hat{U}_t$ and $\hat{V}_t$, to test the hypothesis of no causality in variance.

Next, we compute the sample cross-correlation coefficient at lag i, $\hat{r}_{UV}(i)$, from the consistent estimates of the conditional mean and variance of X_t and Y_t. This gives us

$$\hat{r}_{UV}(i) = C_{UV}(i)(C_{UU}(0)C_{VV}(0))^{-0.5}, \tag{14}$$

where $C_{UV}(i)$ is the ith lag sample cross-covariance, given by

$$C_{UV}(i) = T^{-1}\sum\left(\hat{U}_t - \bar{\hat{U}}\right)\left(\hat{V}_{t-i} - \bar{\hat{V}}\right), \quad i = 0, \pm1, \pm2, \ldots, \tag{15}$$

and, similarly, where $C_{UU}(0)$ and $C_{VV}(0)$ are defined as the sample variance of U_t and V_t, respectively.

Causality in variance of X_t and Y_t can be tested by examining the squared standardized residual CCF, $\hat{r}_{UV}(i)$. Under the condition of regularity, it holds that

$$\begin{pmatrix} \sqrt{T}\hat{r}_{UV}(i) \\ \sqrt{T}\hat{r}_{UV}(i') \end{pmatrix} \xrightarrow{L} AN\left(\begin{bmatrix} 0 \\ 1 \end{bmatrix}, \begin{bmatrix} 1 & 0 \\ 0 & 1 \end{bmatrix}\right), \quad i \neq i'. \tag{16}$$

This test statistic can be used to test the null hypothesis of no causality in variance. To test for a causal relationship at a specified lag i, we compare $\hat{r}_{UV}(i)$ with the standard normal distribution. If the test statistic is larger than the critical value of the normal distribution, we reject the null hypothesis.

4.4 Data

For the empirical analysis, this research used daily data of the Indian stock index and net FII flows into India. The BSE SENSEX 30, India's leading index, provided the data for the stock prices, which was obtained from Datastream. Here, net FII is defined as the value of FII inflows to India minus FII outflows from the country. This information was provided by the Web site of the Securities and Exchange Board of India (SEBI) (http://www.sebi.gov.in/sebiweb/).

Both the cumulative net FII flows and the end-of-the-month BSE SENSEX 30 have followed upward trends since around April/May 2003 (Figure 4.1). This coincidence may be explained as a partial reflection of high economic growth experienced by the country and the improved performance of listed companies. Real gross domestic product growth increased from 3.8% in FY 2002 to 8.5% in FY 2003 and is currently in the 7.0–9.0% range. Since FY 2003, listed companies have also improved their profitability, especially in terms of sales growth, value of production, and gross profits.

Moreover, the Finance Bill 2003, passed by the *Lok Sabha* (the lower house of the Parliament of India) on April 30, 2003, stated that the capital gains arising from all listed equities acquired on or after March 1, 2003 and sold after a year or more shall be exempted from tax. This legislation is also thought to have prompted increased investments in Indian equities.

As discussed above, there may have been a structural break after the second quarter of 2003. To test for this, the entire sampled period, from January 1, 1999 to March 31, 2008, was split into two periods (January 1, 1999 to April 30, 2003 and May 1, 2003 to March 31, 2008) to ascertain whether there was a structural change in FII and stock price movements. The first period corresponds roughly to the sample period in the reviewed studies.

To check the properties of the data, an augmented Dickey–Fuller (ADF) test was conducted for each variable for each period (Dickey and Fuller, 1979).[4] The results indicate that net FII does not have a unit root at the conventional level. Further, while the stock price has a unit root at the conventional level, it does not have a unit root in the first difference. Therefore, net FII was found to be stationary and the stock price was integrated at the order of one.

4.5 Empirical Results

4.5.1 Causality test based on the LA-VAR

As mentioned previously, Chakrabarti (2001) and Mukherjee *et al.* (2002) found a unidirectional relationship from Indian stock returns to FII flows by applying a pairwise Granger causality test. Using more recent data, this section re-examines the causal relationship between these variables in the Granger sense. Thus, the causality test conducted here differs from that employed in the reviewed studies and is based on the LA-VAR method from Toda and Yamamoto (1995).

The conventional asymptotic theory is not applicable to hypothesis testing of VAR in levels, if the variables are integrated or cointegrated. Thus, in estimating the VAR, it is generally required to test whether the variables are integrated, cointegrated, or stationary, by the unit root and cointegration tests (Toda and Yamamoto, 1995, pp. 225–226). On the other hand, a unit root test is not powerful enough for hypothesis testing while the cointegration test is not very reliable for small samples. In order to avoid these potential biases, we apply the LA-VAR method. It becomes possible to test the coefficient restrictions of the VAR in levels, without paying attention to the properties in the economic time series, such as a unit root and cointegration, but adding a priori maximum integration order (d_{max}) to the true lag length (k).

---

[4]A Phillips–Perron test was also conducted as an alternative unit root test, which confirmed the unchanged results of the ADF test (results available upon request).

The Granger causality test based on the LA-VAR method was carried out in the following way. First, the VAR in levels was estimated using ordinary least squares, and the true lag length (k) was selected on the basis of the Akaike Information Criterion (AIC) developed by Akaike (1974). Thus, values of $k = 12$ and $k = 20$ were used for the first and the second period, respectively.[5] Next, d_{max} was set as either 1 or 2, and the model was estimated again with the lags $k + d_{max}$. Finally, the null hypothesis of Granger non-causality was tested using the Wald test. Asymptotically, the Wald test statistic has a chi-squared distribution, with degrees of freedom equal to the excluded number of lagged variables.

Table 4.1 indicates the Wald test statistic for each sample period in the case of $d_{max} = 1$. In the first period, there is a causal relationship from the stock price to FII, whereas in the second period, the bidirectional causality is statistically significant at the conventional level. To check the robustness of the empirical results, Table 4.2 presents the Wald test statistic for each sample period, using $d_{max} = 2$ and statistically confirms the same results as

Table 4.1   Causality from LA-VAR ($d_{max} = 1$)

	Explanatory Variables	
Explained Variables	Stock Returns	FII
Period: January 1, 1999 to April 30, 2003		
Stock Returns	—	18.924
FII	103.884**	—
Period: May 1, 2003 to March 31, 2008		
Stock Returns	—	39.337**
FII	342.758**	—

Notes: (1) The numbers are the Wald test statistic.
(2) ** indicates that the null hypothesis of Granger non-causality is rejected at the 1% significance level.

---

[5]The true lag length (k) was determined from a maximum of 20 lag numbers. The Lagrange multiplier test showed that the null hypothesis of no autocorrelation up to 20 lags is accepted at the conventional level. Therefore, the model specification is empirically supported in terms of the maximum lag numbers.

Table 4.2   Causality from LA-VAR ($d_{max} = 2$)

Explained Variables	Explanatory Variables	
	Stock Returns	FII
Period: January 1, 1999 to April 30, 2003		
Stock Returns	—	18.568
FII	102.115**	—
Period: May 1, 2003 to March 31, 2008		
Stock Returns	—	42.275**
FII	336.730**	—

Notes: (1) The numbers are the Wald test statistic.
(2) ** indicates that the null hypothesis of Granger non-causality is rejected at the 1% significance level.

those of Table 4.1. To sum up, the findings are consistent with those from the literature. Thus, there was a unidirectional relationship from stock prices to FII flows during the period 1999 to 2003, while the sample period beginning in 2003 witnessed a bidirectional relationship between stock prices and net FII. These results also indicate that a structural break occurred in mid-2003.

4.5.2   Causality test based on the CCF approach

The CCF approach used here was developed by Cheung and Ng (1996) to examine the causal relationships in the mean and variance between two variables. The first step is to estimate the univariate time series model for each variable that allows for time variation in both the conditional mean and the conditional variance. Unlike Cheung and Ng (1996), who adopted the Generalized Autoregressive Conditional Heteroscedasticity (GARCH) model, an AR-exponential GARCH (AR-EGARCH) model was applied here to obtain the conditional mean and the conditional variance for the concerned variable, that is, y_t.[6] Equations (17) and (18) are the AR (m) and

---

[6]See Nelson (1991). Hamori (2003) summarized the advantages of the EGARCH model over the standard GARCH model.

EGARCH (1,1) models, respectively.

$$y_t = \pi_0 + \sum_{i=1}^{m} \pi_i y_{t-i} + \varepsilon_t, \quad \varepsilon_t | I_{t-1} \sim N(0, \delta_t^2), \quad (17)$$

$$\log \delta_t^2 = \varphi + \alpha \left| \frac{\varepsilon_{t-1}}{\delta_{t-1}} \right| + \beta \log(\delta_{t-1}^2) + \gamma \frac{\varepsilon_{t-1}}{\delta_{t-1}}, \quad (18)$$

where π_0 and φ are constants, ε_t is the error term, δ_t^2 is the conditional variance of ε_t, and z_t is independent and identically distributed with zero mean and unit variance. Both z_t and δ_t are statistically independent and $z_t = \varepsilon_t / \delta_t$.

Since y_t is assumed to be stationary, the empirical analysis used net FII flows and return on stock. The latter is defined as the stock price difference from the previous trading day. Tables 4.3 and 4.4 indicate the estimation results of the AR-EGARCH model, that is, the maximum-likelihood estimates and their standard errors, for each variable in the first period and the second period, respectively. Based on the AIC and residual diagnostics, the appropriate lag-order of the AR model was determined from a maximum of 20 lag numbers. Table 4.3 shows that AR(9)-EGARCH(1,1) was selected during the first period, while Table 4.4 shows that AR(10)-EGARCH(1,1) was selected during the second period. It can be seen that the coefficients of the ARCH term (α) and the GARCH term (β) are statistically significant at the 1% level, but the coefficients of the asymmetric effect (γ) are insignificant in all cases.[7]

In the second step of the CCF approach, the standardized residuals and their squares were obtained from the estimates of the conditional means and variances in the first step, and the causality in mean and the causality in variance were tested based on the sample cross-correlation coefficients.

Table 4.5 shows the test statistic, $\sqrt{T}\hat{r}_{\varepsilon\xi}(i)$, to test the null hypothesis of no causality in mean in both periods. The term "Lag" in the table refers to the number of periods in which stock returns lag FII flows, while "Lead"

---

[7]Tables 4.3 and 4.4 also show the Ljung–Box test statistics, $Q(20)$ and $Q^2(20)$. These indicated that the null hypothesis of no autocorrelation up to the order 20 is accepted for both standardized residuals and their squares in all cases. Therefore, the diagnostic results statistically support the specification of the selected AR-EGARCH models.

Table 4.3   Empirical Results of the AR-EGARCH Model (January 1, 1999 to April 30, 2003)

AR(m):
$$y_t = \pi_0 + \sum_{i=1}^{m} \pi_i y_{t-i} + \varepsilon_t$$

EGARCH(1,1):
$$\log \delta_t^2 = \varphi + \alpha \left| \frac{\varepsilon_{t-1}}{\delta_{t-1}} \right| + \beta \log(\delta_{t-1}^2) + \gamma \frac{\varepsilon_{t-1}}{\delta_{t-1}}$$

Variable	Stock Returns		FII	
	AR(9)-EGARCH(1,1)		AR(9)-EGARCH(1,1)	
Model	Estimates	SE	Estimates	SE
AR(m)				
π_0	−0.321	1.512	9.268**	2.782
π_1	0.048	0.033	0.210**	0.043
π_2	0.009	0.038	0.128**	0.036
π_3	0.026	0.033	0.048	0.031
π_4	0.078*	0.031	−0.009	0.038
π_5	−0.024	0.036	0.043	0.034
π_6	−0.070*	0.034	−0.023	0.038
π_7	0.005	0.032	−0.013	0.044
π_8	0.034	0.034	0.066*	0.031
π_9	0.075*	0.032	0.053	0.037
EGARCH(1,1)				
φ	−0.047	0.049	0.084	0.059
α	0.193**	0.051	0.130**	0.034
β	0.988**	0.006	0.982**	0.006
γ	−0.056	0.350	−0.087	0.077
Log Likelihood	−5847.192		−6441.295	
p-value of $Q(20)$	0.230		0.715	
p-value of $Q^2(20)$	0.962		0.904	

Notes: (1) Significance at the 1% and 5% level is indicated by ** and *, respectively.
(2) Both $Q(20)$ and $Q^2(20)$ are Ljung–Box test statistics for the null hypothesis that there is no autocorrelation up to the order 20 for standardized residuals and their squares, respectively. If the p-value is less than 0.01 and/or 0.05, the null hypothesis is rejected at the 1% and 5% level, respectively.
(3) SE indicates the Bollerslev–Wooldridge robust standard errors, which are robust to departures from normality.

Table 4.4   Empirical Results of the AR-EGARCH Model (May 1, 2003 to March 31, 2008)

AR(m):
$$y_t = \pi_0 + \sum_{i=1}^{m} \pi_i y_{t-i} + \varepsilon_t$$

EGARCH(1,1):
$$\log \delta_t^2 = \varphi + \alpha \left| \frac{\varepsilon_{t-1}}{\delta_{t-1}} \right| + \beta \log(\delta_{t-1}^2) + \gamma \frac{\varepsilon_{t-1}}{\delta_{t-1}}$$

Variable	Stock Returns		FII	
	AR(10)-EGARCH(1,1)		AR(10)-EGARCH(1,1)	
Model	Estimates	SE	Estimates	SE
AR(m)				
π_0	9.447**	2.285	32.185**	10.917
π_1	0.116**	0.031	0.350**	0.052
π_2	−0.056	0.032	−0.016	0.066
π_3	0.051	0.034	0.193**	0.049
π_4	−0.011	0.029	0.048	0.044
π_5	−0.046	0.033	0.011	0.037
π_6	−0.056	0.031	0.010	0.048
π_7	0.034	0.029	−0.082	0.054
π_8	−0.036	0.029	0.083*	0.034
π_9	0.030	0.031	0.007	0.038
π_{10}	0.068*	0.032	0.103	0.053
EGARCH(1,1)				
φ	−0.117*	0.052	0.102	0.122
α	0.307*	0.047	0.411**	0.070
β	0.988**	0.005	0.970**	0.010
γ	−0.036	0.034	0.005	0.050
Log Likelihood	−7513.057		−9149.406	
p-value of $Q(20)$	0.994		0.294	
p-value of $Q^2(20)$	0.843		0.999	

Notes: (1) Significance at the 1% and 5% level is indicated by ** and *, respectively.
(2) Both $Q(20)$ and $Q^2(20)$ are Ljung–Box test statistics for the null hypothesis that there is no autocorrelation up to the order of 20 for standardized residuals and their squares, respectively. If the p-value is less than 0.01 and/or 0.05, the null hypothesis is rejected at the 1% and 5% level, respectively.
(3) SE indicates the Bollerslev–Wooldridge robust standard errors, which are robust to departures from normality.

Indian Economy

Table 4.5   Causality in the Mean between FII Flows and Stock Returns

| | First Period (January 1, 1999 to April 30, 2003) | | Second Period (May 1, 2003 to March 31, 2008) | |
| | Lag | Lead | Lag | Lead |
Lag or Lead i	Stock Returns and FII $(-i)$	Stock Returns and FII $(+i)$	Stock Returns and FII $(-i)$	Stock Returns and FII $(+i)$
0	0.070*		0.014	
1	0.023	0.255**	0.039	0.310**
2	−0.013	0.139**	−0.006	0.170**
3	0.022	−0.017	−0.001	0.040
4	−0.042	−0.068*	0.027	0.002
5	0.018	0.000	0.007	−0.010
6	−0.001	0.012	0.003	0.009
7	−0.011	0.014	0.028	−0.012
8	−0.011	−0.009	−0.023	0.059*
9	−0.027	−0.013	−0.053	−0.014
10	0.032	−0.062*	−0.001	−0.056*
11	0.041	−0.017	0.012	0.038
12	−0.008	−0.039	0.014	−0.044
13	0.007	−0.038	0.000	−0.026
14	−0.051	−0.020	−0.030	−0.007
15	0.003	−0.020	0.013	−0.006
16	0.032	−0.001	0.008	−0.059*
17	−0.053	−0.026	−0.019	−0.021
18	−0.005	0.029	−0.015	−0.011
19	−0.021	0.048	−0.006	−0.005
20	−0.025	−0.053	0.060*	0.017
21	−0.030	−0.027	0.027	−0.012
22	0.038	−0.037	0.023	0.034
23	0.006	−0.031	−0.065*	−0.007
24	−0.024	0.030	−0.011	0.032
25	0.007	0.017	−0.069*	−0.018
26	−0.025	−0.006	0.002	0.023
27	0.057	−0.033	0.008	−0.024
28	−0.039	0.050	−0.051	−0.019
29	−0.011	−0.010	−0.030	−0.013
30	−0.037	0.050	−0.052	−0.009

Note: Significance at the 1% and 5% level is indicated by ** and *, respectively.

refers to the number of periods the returns lead FII flows. Significant test statistic at a specific number of lags (i) implies that the return on stock influences net FII at that point. Similarly, the significant test statistic at a specific number of leads (i) implies that net FII influences stock returns at that point. Table 4.5 shows that during the first period, FII flows did not affect stock returns. However, stock returns affected FII flows at lags 1, 2, 4, and 10. On the other hand, during the second period, FII flows affected stock returns at lags 20, 23, and 25, while stock returns affected FII flows at lags 1, 2, 8, 10, and 16.

Similarly, Table 4.6 shows the test statistic, $\sqrt{T}\hat{r}_{\varepsilon\xi}(i)$, to test the null hypothesis of no causality in variance in both periods. It is clear that during the first period, FII flows did not influence stock returns. However, stock returns influenced FII flows at lag 2. On the other hand, during the second period, FII flows influenced stock returns at lag 19, while stock returns influenced FII flows at lag 1.

To sum up, the results show that the return on stock unidirectionally caused FII flows in both the mean and the variance during the first period, while the return on stock and FII flows were found to induce each other in both the mean and the variance during the second period. On focusing on the evidence during the second period, it can be seen that FII flows, induced stock returns after longer time intervals than stock returns induced FII flows, which is common for causality in mean and causality in variance.

4.6 Concluding Remarks

Since mid-2003, the significant increase in FII inflow into India has made it the primary source of portfolio investment. Given the dominant role of equity in FII flows and the low level of floating stocks, the surge of FII inflows is widely considered to have affected stock price movements in the country; the stock index has shown a significant upward movement since mid-2003. While studies have been conducted on this topic, they were done prior to this upward movement. Moreover, these studies used daily and/or monthly data from before 2003, and only found an impact from stock returns on FII flows. In contrast, this work re-examined the causal relationship between net FII flows and Indian stock returns before and after 2003. It used daily data from January 1, 1999 to April 30, 2003 to

Table 4.6   Causality in the Variance between FII Flows and Stock Returns

Lag or Lead i	First Period (January 1, 1999 to April 30, 2003)		Second Period (May 1, 2003 to March 31, 2008)	
	Lag	Lead	Lag	Lead
	Stock Returns and FII $(-i)$	Stock Returns and FII $(+i)$	Stock Returns and FII $(-i)$	Stock Returns and FII $(+i)$
0	0.000		−0.045	
1	0.041	0.012	0.014	0.087**
2	0.000	0.072*	0.034	0.020
3	−0.005	0.036	−0.010	−0.030
4	−0.006	−0.012	0.030	−0.023
5	0.001	−0.010	0.013	−0.019
6	−0.012	0.021	−0.023	0.004
7	0.015	0.007	−0.023	0.002
8	−0.022	0.002	0.013	−0.012
9	0.000	−0.006	−0.016	0.029
10	−0.007	−0.009	0.016	0.000
11	−0.014	−0.028	−0.013	0.035
12	−0.015	0.000	−0.024	0.010
13	−0.013	0.014	0.028	0.009
14	−0.005	0.015	−0.004	0.034
15	0.015	−0.013	0.054	0.019
16	−0.018	−0.019	−0.038	0.021
17	0.006	0.001	0.040	−0.020
18	−0.013	−0.018	0.000	0.003
19	0.015	0.047	0.145**	−0.014
20	0.015	−0.013	−0.029	−0.011
21	0.004	−0.024	0.016	0.009
22	0.032	−0.005	0.036	−0.012
23	−0.016	−0.022	0.022	−0.036
24	−0.011	−0.001	0.054	−0.005
25	−0.022	−0.021	0.023	−0.015
26	−0.020	−0.015	−0.032	−0.004
27	−0.017	−0.008	−0.019	0.000
28	−0.003	0.018	0.054	−0.017
29	−0.013	−0.007	0.012	0.004
30	−0.016	−0.015	−0.019	−0.019

Note: Significance at the 1% and 5% level is indicated by ** and *, respectively.

re-examine the first period, and data from May 1, 2003 to March 31, 2008 to analyze the second period.

The analysis used two empirical techniques: the CCF approach and the LA-VAR based causality test. The results of the CCF approach show that, from May 2003, there has been a bidirectional relationship between stock returns and FII flows, both in the mean and the variance. Moreover, there was a unidirectional causal relationship from stock returns to FII flows, both in the mean and the variance before May 2003. This indicates that causality from stock returns to FII flows has taken place in both sample periods, whereas the causality from FII flows to stock returns was existent in the latter period only. In terms of the causal directions, the LA-VAR based Granger causality test supports the results of the CCF approach, thus indicating the robustness of the empirical results.

Moreover, on focusing on the results of the CCF approach post-2003, it can be seen that FII flows have caused stock returns after longer time intervals than stock returns have caused FII flows, for both the causality in mean and the causality in variance. This means that stock price changes quickly affect foreign investor behavior, whereas FII flows take more time to affect stock returns. This is probably because of other macroeconomic variables, such as interest rates, asset prices, reserves, money supply, and inflation (RBI, 1996, p. 61).

In sum, the findings of this chapter, especially those pertaining to the latter period, suggest that net FII inflows have continued to exert an impact on the movement of Indian stock prices, albeit at longer intervals. Over the last five years, net FII inflows have generally trended upward with the movement of stock prices in India. After the peak in mid-January 2008, however, there were significant reversals in this trend; FII inflows turned into persistent outflows, and stock prices decreased at a record pace. Under these circumstances, the results of this work lead us to conclude that when the authorities monitor the movement of future stock prices, they should pay more attention to FII flows than they did in the past. Furthermore, in view of the growing role of FII flow in India's stock market and its potentially destabilizing nature, the authorities would do well to create an environment in which foreign investors would like to keep holding onto the stock with confidence. As an example, it is recommended to enhance the credibility of the Indian equity market by strengthening firms' disclosure and corporate governance procedures on the one hand and the predictability of changes in FII regulations on the other.

References

Akaike, H., 1974. A new look at the statistical model identification. *IEEE Transactions on Automatic Control* AC-19, 716–723.

Chakrabarti, R., 2001. FII flows to India: Nature and causes. *ICRA Bulletin Money & Finance* October–December, 61–81.

Cheung, Y.W., Ng, L.K., 1996. A causality-in-variance test and its application to financial market prices. *Journal of Econometrics* 72, 33–48.

Committee on the Global Financial System, 2009. Capital flows and emerging market economies. BIS CGFS Papers 33, Bank for International Settlements, Basel.

Dickey, D.A., Fuller, W.A., 1979. Distribution of the estimators for autoregressive time series with a unit root. *Journal of the American Statistical Association* 74, 427–431.

Gordon, J., Gupta, P., 2003. Portfolio flows into India: Do domestic fundamentals matter? IMF Working Paper WP/03/20, International Monetary Fund, Washington, DC.

Griffin, J.M., Nardari, F., Stulz, R.M., 2002. Daily cross-border equity flows: Pushed or pulled? NBER Working Paper Series 9000, The National Bureau of Economic Research, Cambridge, MA.

Hamori, S., 2003. *An Empirical Investigation of Stock Markets: The CCF Approach*. Kluwer Academic, Boston.

Hong, Y., 2001. A test for volatility spillover with application to exchange rate. *Journal of Econometrics* 103, 183–224.

International Monetary Fund (IMF), 2009. *International Financial Statistics, June*. IMF, Washington, DC.

Mukherjee, P., Bose, S., Coondoo, D., 2002. Foreign institutional investment in the Indian equity market: An analysis of daily flows during January 1999–May 2002. *ICRA Bulletin Money & Finance* April–September, 21–51.

Nelson, D.B., 1991. Conditional heteroskedasticity in asset returns: A new approach. *Econometrica* 59, 347–370.

Reserve Bank of India (RBI), 1996. *Annual Report 1995–96*. RBI, Mumbai.

Reserve Bank of India (RBI), 2008a. *Annual Report 2007–08*. RBI, Mumbai.

Reserve Bank of India (RBI), 2008b. *Handbook of Statistics on Indian Economy 2007–08*. RBI, Mumbai.

Toda, H.Y., Yamamoto, T., 1995. Statistical inference in vector autoregressions with possibly integrated processes. *Journal of Econometrics* 66, 225–250.

Chapter 5

Market Efficiency of Commodity Futures in India

5.1 Introduction

Following repeated changes in the rules and regulations by the authorities, the Indian commodity futures market has witnessed a surge in values and volumes of traded commodities over the last decade. The history of commodity futures in India can be traced back to the end of the 19th century when the Bombay Cotton Trade Association established cotton contracts. In the interwar period, the futures market underwent rapid growth, although futures trading was prohibited during the Second World War under the Defence of India Act (FMC, 2011a, p. 1). After its transient resumption and prosperity in the mid-1950s, futures trading was again banned in 1966 except for a few minor commodities; thereafter, it was practically deactivated. During the 1980s, commodity futures trading was partially permitted in a few commodities, but it was in the liberalization process beginning in 1991 that the Indian government reassessed the role of commodity futures trading in the economy.

In 2003, the government lifted the prohibition against futures trading in all commodities and recognized the establishment of three electronic exchanges — the National Multi Commodity Exchange of India, the Multi Commodity Exchange of India (MCX), and the National Commodity and Derivatives Exchange (NCDEX) — as national level multi-commodity exchanges (FMC, 2011a, p. 6). Moreover, the Indian Commodity Exchange and the Ace Derivatives and Commodity Exchange were also granted recognition as the fourth and fifth national multi-commodity exchanges in India

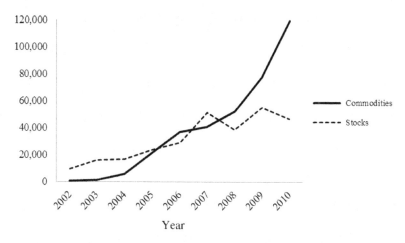

Figure 5.1 Total Value of Commodities and Stocks in India (Rs. Billion)
Source: FMC (2011a, 2011b), MOCAFPD (various issues), and SEBI (2012).

in 2009 and 2010, respectively. With the establishment of these exchanges, the commodity futures market witnessed massive growth in India. The total value of commodities traded steadily increased, and, on reaching Rs. 52.49 trillion in FY 2008, outperformed the domestic stock market (see Figure 5.1). Certainly, the commodity market has grown to become one of the major financial markets in India.

Generally, the futures market is believed to have two important economic functions, price risk management and price discovery. In price risk management, both the producers and consumers manage their price risks in the spot market by taking equal but opposite positions in the futures market; this is called the hedging of price risks in commodities. Besides these market participants whose aim is to hedge against price risks, there are certain other parties in the futures market whose aim is to undertake risks and earn profits by doing so (Easwaran and Ramasundaram, 2008, p. 339). Since the futures market participants come with various objectives and different data, the market enables the current futures price to indicate accurately the spot price expected at the maturity of the futures contracts. This is referred to as the price discovery function of the futures market. Only an efficient futures market can perform these functions. As proposed by Fama (1970), we consider a market weak-form efficient if its futures prices reflect all the available information for predicting the future spot prices but the participants are unable to consistently make profits.[1]

In this chapter, we focus on India, a developing country with phenomenal growth in its commodity market, and empirically examine whether the market efficiency hypothesis holds in the Indian commodity market. More specifically, we first estimate the long-run equilibrium relationship between multi-commodity futures and spot prices and then test for market efficiency in a weak-form sense by applying both the dynamic ordinary least squares (DOLS) (Saikkonen, 1992; Stock and Watson, 1993) and fully modified ordinary least squares (FMOLS) (Phillips and Hansen, 1990) methods.

The remainder of this chapter is organized as follows. Section 5.2 briefly reviews the relevant literature and discusses the contributions of this study. Section 5.3 presents our model, and Section 5.4 explains the empirical techniques used. Section 5.5 provides the definitions, sources, and properties of the data, and Section 5.6 gives the empirical results of the study. Section 5.7, the final section, summarizes our main findings and suggests policy implications.

5.2 Literature Review

Since the introduction of cointegration theory, according to which two variables are said to be cointegrated if they move closely together over time, a growing body of literature has empirically tested market efficiency of commodity futures around the world. If the non-stationary spot and futures prices are cointegrated, a long-run equilibrium relationship can be said to exist between them. However, if these two price series are not cointegrated, they diverge without bound, such that the futures price would provide little information regarding the movement of the spot price (Lai and Lai, 1991, p. 569). Therefore, cointegration between the spot and the futures prices is a necessary condition for market efficiency (*ibid.*, 1991, p. 568). Market

---

[1]Fama (1970) classified market efficiency into three categories: weak-form efficiency, semi-strong-form efficiency, and strong-form efficiency. Unlike weak-form efficiency, semi-strong efficiency indicates that all public information is calculated into the current prices, while strong-form efficiency indicates that all information in a market, whether public or private, is accounted for in prices.

efficiency also requires that the futures price is an unbiased predictor — on average — of spot prices, thereby indicating that these two price indices have a cointegrating vector $(1, -1)$.

Thus far, empirical analyses on market efficiency of commodity futures have been conducted mainly for developed countries.[2] The examples include Chowdhury (1991) and Kellard (2002) for the United Kingdom, and Beck (1994) and McKenzie *et al.* (2002) for the United States. Meanwhile, relevant studies for developing countries are growing significantly but are still limited. For examples of the studies on countries other than India, we have Wang and Ke (2005) and Xin *et al.* (2006), both of which examined the efficiency of the Chinese commodity market using cointegration methods.

The few early studies on India include Bose (2008), Goyari and Jena (2011), and Jabir and Gupta (2011).[3] Bose (2008) examined some features of the Indian commodity futures in order to examine whether the commodity prices fulfill market efficiency functions. For her analysis, Bose used different methods such as correlation, cointegration, and causality as well as data of price indices from the MCX and the NCDEX from June 2005 to September 2007. The results of her study show that multi-commodity futures indices help to reduce volatility in the spot prices of corresponding commodities and provide for the effective hedging of price risks; however, agricultural indices do not exhibit these features clearly.

Further, Jabir and Gupta (2011) analyzed the efficiency of 12 agricultural commodity markets by examining the relationships between the futures and spot prices from 2004 to 2007. They used cointegration and causality tests, and the results indicate that cointegration existed in the indices of all commodities except wheat and rice and that the direction of causality is mixed, depending on the commodity.

Finally, Goyari and Jena (2011) examined the commodity futures market from June 2005 to January 2008 using the daily spot and futures prices of gold, crude oil, and guar seed. Their cointegration test results show that

---

[2]The formal futures market was originated in the Osaka rice market during Japan's Tokugawa Era (see Schaede (1989) and Hamori *et al.* (2001)).

[3]Easwaran and Ramasundaram (2008) and Vishwanathan and Pillai (2010) examined the Indian commodity futures market by using techniques other than cointegration.

the spot and futures prices of these three commodities are cointegrated, suggesting that they have a long-run relationship.

As mentioned above, all these studies use the period before 2008 as their sample period and thus, do not examine the period during which the Indian commodity futures gained significant momentum. Furthermore, these studies conduct the Johansen cointegration test, but do not test the cointegrating parameter restriction for the unbiasedness hypothesis. This hypothesis implies that the current futures price of a commodity should equal its future spot price at contract maturity (McKenzie *et al.*, 2002, p. 478). In this study, we address both these aspects — therein lies the unique contribution of this study to the existing literature.

5.3 Model

The basic model used in this study is specified as follows:

$$\ln(S_t) = \alpha + \beta(F_t) + u_t, \tag{1}$$

where S_t is the spot index, F_t is the futures index, α is the risk premium, and u_t is the error term. We estimate Equation (1) using two alternative methods — the FMOLS and the DOLS — to test the efficiency of the commodity futures market in India: if $\beta = 1$, the market is efficient. The null and alternative hypotheses are specified respectively in the following manner: $H_0 : \beta = 1, H_A : \beta \neq 1$.

5.4 Empirical Techniques

To estimate the cointegrating vector, Phillips and Hansen (1990) proposed a single-equation method based on ordinary least squares (OLS) with semi-parametric correction for serial correlation and endogeneity, which is FMOLS. Let the dependent variable be denoted by y_t and the vector of regressors by x_t, where x_t is an $m \times 1$ vector and $t = 1, 2, \ldots, T$. The behavior of y_t and x_t is assumed to satisfy

$$y_t = x_t'\beta + d_t'\alpha + u_{1t}, \tag{2}$$

$$x_t = x_{t-1} + u_{2t}, \tag{3}$$

where d_t is a vector of deterministic trend regressors. Let $u_t = (u_{1t}, u'_{2t})'$ be a joint innovation process; then, the one-sided long-run covariance matrix Λ and long-run covariance matrix Ω can be expressed as follows:

$$\Lambda = \sum_{i=0}^{\infty} E(u_t u'_{t-i}) = \begin{bmatrix} \lambda_{11} & \lambda_{12} \\ \lambda_{21} & \Lambda_{22} \end{bmatrix}, \tag{4}$$

$$\Omega = \sum_{i=-\infty}^{\infty} E(u_t u'_{t-i}) = \begin{bmatrix} \omega_{11} & \omega_{12} \\ \omega_{21} & \Omega_{22} \end{bmatrix}. \tag{5}$$

Let $y_t^+ = y_t - \hat{\omega}_{12}\hat{\Omega}_{22}^{-1}\Delta x_t$ and $\hat{\lambda}_{12}^+ = \hat{\lambda}_{12} - \hat{\omega}_{12}\hat{\Omega}_{22}^{-1}\hat{\Lambda}_{22}$, where $\hat{\lambda}_{12}, \hat{\omega}_{12}, \hat{\Omega}_{22}^{-1}$ and $\hat{\Lambda}_{22}$ are consistent estimates of the respective parameters. The FMOLS estimator is given by

$$\begin{bmatrix} \hat{\beta} \\ \hat{\alpha} \end{bmatrix} = \left(\sum_{t=1}^{T} z_t z'_t \right)^{-1} \left(\sum_{t=1}^{T} z_t y_t^+ - T \begin{bmatrix} \hat{\lambda}_{12}^{+'} \\ 0 \end{bmatrix} \right), \tag{6}$$

where $z_t = (x'_t, d'_t)'$.

Saikkonen (1992) and Stock and Watson (1993) proposed DOLS as a simple efficient estimator. The DOLS specification simply adds leads and lags of the first difference of stochastic regressors to the standard cointegrating regression:

$$y_t = x'_t \beta + d'_t \alpha + \sum_{i=-K}^{K} \Delta x'_{t+i} \gamma + v_t. \tag{7}$$

Obtained from Equation (7), the DOLS estimator $(\hat{\beta}', \hat{\alpha}')'$, has the same asymptotic distribution as those obtained from FMOLS.

5.5 Data

Unlike previous studies using individual agricultural commodities, this investigation uses multi-commodity price indices, that is, the spot index (MCXSCOMDEX) and futures index (MCXCOMDEX) obtained from the MCX Web site (http://www.mcxindia.com/). Figure 5.2 depicts the movements of the closing prices of MCXSCOMDEX and MCXCOMDEX, respectively. The sample period for this study is from January 2006 to

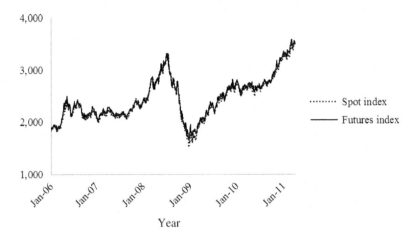

Figure 5.2   The Movements of Commodity Price Indices
Source: Compiled by the authors from the MCX Web site (http://www.mcxindia.com/).

Table 5.1   Unit Root Tests

Variable	Specification	Test Statistic	*p*-value
LS	Constant and Trend	−1.487	0.834
	Constant	−0.954	0.771
LF	Constant and Trend	−1.471	0.839
	Constant	−0.878	0.796
ΔLS	Constant	−39.161	0.000
	None	−39.129	0.000
ΔLF	Constant	−39.929	0.000
	None	−39.893	0.000

Note: LS is the logarithm of the multi-commodity spot price index. LF is the logarithm of the multi-commodity futures price index. Δ represents the first difference.

March 2011. We use the daily data for this period, and the total number of observations is 1,590.

To confirm our data properties, we conduct a unit root test for the natural logarithm of each price. Table 5.1 presents the results of the augmented Dickey–Fuller test (Dickey and Fuller, 1979). The table clearly shows that the level of each variable has a unit root, while the first difference of each variable does not have a unit root. Therefore, we can conclude that each index is a non-stationary variable with a unit root.

Table 5.2   Cointegration Tests

Number of Lags	Test	Null Hypothesis	Test Statistic	p-value
1	Trace	$r = 0$	365.491	0.000
		$r = 1$	0.793	0.373
	Max Eigenvalue	$r = 0$	364.699	0.000
		$r = 1$	0.793	0.373
2	Trace	$r = 0$	127.191	0.000
		$r = 1$	0.880	0.348
	Max Eigenvalue	$r = 0$	126.311	0.000
		$r = 1$	0.880	0.348
3	Trace	$r = 0$	67.735	0.000
		$r = 1$	1.118	0.290
	Max Eigenvalue	$r = 0$	66.617	0.000
		$r = 1$	1.118	0.290

Notes: (1) Lag order indicates the number of lags for the difference vector autoregression (VAR) system.
(2) r indicates the number of cointegrating vectors under the null hypothesis.

Next, we conduct the Johansen cointegration test for the indices of spot and future prices (Johansen and Juselius, 1990; Johansen, 1991). There are two kinds of Johansen-type tests: the trace test and the maximum eigenvalue test. Table 5.2 presents the results of the cointegration test. Here, we use lags 1, 2, and 3 to check the robustness of our empirical results. As is evident from this table, the null hypothesis of no cointegrating relation is rejected in all cases at the 1% level, while the null hypothesis of one cointegrating relation is not rejected in all cases. Therefore, the existence of a cointegrating relation is statistically supported for multi-commodity spot and futures prices.

5.6   Empirical Results

5.6.1   Full-sample analysis

Table 5.3 presents the results of the hypothesis test. As seen in the table, DOLS estimation reveals the value of β as 1.032 and that the null hypothesis of $\beta = 1$ is rejected at the conventional level. The result is the same in the case of the FMOLS. Therefore, we find that the Indian commodity futures

Table 5.3 Cointegration Estimation Results (Full-sample Analysis)
$\ln(S_t) = \alpha + \beta \ln(F_t) + u_t$

	DOLS			FMOLS	
$\hat{\beta}$	t-Statistic ($H_0 : \beta = 0$)	t-Statistic ($H_0 : \beta = 1$)	$\hat{\beta}$	t-Statistic ($H_0 : \beta = 0$)	t-Statistic ($H_0 : \beta = 1$)
1.032	187.251**	5.851**	1.032	188.487**	5.772**

Notes: (1) The number of leads and lags is set to 3 when estimating with DOLS.
(2) ** indicates that the null hypothesis is rejected at the 1% significance level.

market is not efficient when considering the entire 2006 to 2011 sample period.

5.6.2 Sub-sample analysis

Next, we divide the full sample period into three sub-sample periods to check for changes in market efficiency over time. The sub-sample periods are specified as follows:

Sub-sample period A: January 2, 2006–June 30, 2008
Sub-sample period B: July 1, 2008–June 30, 2009
Sub-sample period C: July 1, 2009–March 31, 2011

The sub-sample periods roughly correspond to the trends of the commodity price indices. Specifically, after having increased until mid-2008 (sub-sample A), both indices plummeted in the subsequent year (sub-sample B), and since then (sub-sample C) both have again shown a significant increasing trend.

Table 5.4 presents the results of each sub-sample period. With regard to sub-sample A, the null hypothesis $\beta = 1$ is rejected and the estimated value of β is 1.027 from DOLS and 1.026 from FMOLS. Next, with regard to sub-sample B, the null hypothesis $\beta = 1$ is rejected and the estimated value of β is 1.101 from DOLS and 1.110 from FMOLS. Finally, with regard to sub-sample C, the null hypothesis $\beta = 1$ is not rejected and the estimated value of β is 0.990 from both DOLS and FMOLS.

In short, market efficiency is not satisfied in sub-samples A and B, while it is fulfilled during the more recent sub-sample C period. This suggests

Table 5.4   Cointegration Estimation Results (Sub-sample Analysis)
$\ln(S_t) = \alpha + \beta \ln(F_t) + u_t$

	DOLS			FMOLS	
$\hat{\beta}$	t-Statistic $(H_0 : \beta = 0)$	t-Statistic $(H_0 : \beta = 1)$	$\hat{\beta}$	t-Statistic $(H_0 : \beta = 0)$	t-Statistic $(H_0 : \beta = 1)$
Sub-sample A: January 2, 2006 to June 30, 2008					
1.027	131.475**	3.464**	1.026	129.947**	3.258**
Sub-sample B: July 1, 2008 to June 30, 2009					
1.101	89.085**	8.168**	1.100	91.896**	8.371**
Sub-sample C: July 1, 2009 to March 31, 2011					
0.990	167.591**	−1.623	0.990	168.713 **	−1.679

Notes: (1) The number of leads and lags is set to 3 when estimating with DOLS.
(2) ** indicates that the null hypothesis is rejected at the 1% significance level.

that with development of the commodity futures market in India, market efficiency has increased.

5.7   Concluding Remarks

In this chapter, we empirically analyzed whether the growing Indian commodity futures market satisfies market efficiency using multi-commodity price indices released by the MCX, the largest national commodity exchange in India. For this purpose, we conducted the Johansen cointegration test for spot and futures price indices from January 2006 to March 2011. The results show that there is a cointegrating relationship between spot and futures prices in India, which implies that one of the necessary conditions for market efficiency is satisfied.

With these results, we proceeded to test another necessary condition for market efficiency, the unbiasedness hypothesis. We employed DOLS and FMOLS estimation to perform the hypothesis tests and examined whether the two price indices have a cointegrating vector $(1, -1)$. We found that during the entire sample period, the null hypothesis that the futures price is the unbiased predictor of the spot prices is rejected, implying that the commodity futures market in India is not efficient. Further, with the sample period divided into three sub-samples, the unbiasedness hypothesis is not rejected only for the more recent sample period, that is, from July 2009 to March 2011. Therefore, we conclude that the commodity futures market in India was efficient only during the more recent period.

Thus far, relevant literature has generally analyzed the cointegrating relation between the spot and futures prices of individual agricultural commodities for the period before the phenomenal growth in traded value of commodity futures in India. In fact, the total value of commodities traded has shown significant growth since FY 2008 (see Figure 5.1). In addition, in line with this trend, the commodity price indices have also increased since mid-2009 (see Figure 5.2). The results of our study imply that as the market size expands, the commodity futures market fulfills weak-form efficiency in that the futures price generally operates as an unbiased predictor of the spot price.

In India, whenever the futures price of a commodity increases sharply, it is usually regarded as the result of speculative activity and the authorities tend to impose several regulations. However, considering our results, we conclude that the efficiency of the commodity market has significantly improved with the increase in trade value since 2009, thereby meaning that the Indian futures market performs the functions of both price risk management and price discovery. Therefore, in order to utilize the futures market for fulfilling these functions more efficiently, the Indian government must further enhance its institutional infrastructure for smoother commodity transactions in line with market developments, rather than increase restrictions on commodity transactions.

References

Beck, S.E., 1994. Cointegration and market efficiency in commodities futures markets. *Applied Economics* 26, 249–257.

Bose, S., 2008. Commodity futures market in India: A study of trends in the national multi-commodity indices. *ICRA Bulletin Money & Finance* May, 125–158.

Chowdhury, A.R., 1991. Futures market efficiency: Evidence from cointegration tests. *Journal of Futures Markets* 11, 577–589.

Dickey, D.A., Fuller, W.A., 1979. Distribution of the estimators for autoregressive time series with a unit root. *Journal of the American Statistical Association* 74, 427–431.

Easwaran, R.S., Ramasundaram, P., 2008. Whether commodity futures market in agriculture is efficient in price discovery? An econometric analysis. *Agricultural Economics Research Review* 21, 337–344.

Fama, E.F., 1970. Efficient capital markets: A review of theory and empirical work. *Journal of Finance* 25, 383–417.

Forward Markets Commission (FMC), 2011a. *Annual Report 2009–10*. FMC, Mumbai.

Forward Markets Commission (FMC), 2011b. *Annual Report 2010–11*. FMC, Mumbai.

Goyari, P., Jena, P.K., 2011. Commodity futures market in India: An econometric analysis. *The Indian Journal of Economics* 92, 699–717.

Hamori, S., Hamori, N., Anderson, D.A., 2001. An empirical analysis of the efficiency of the Osaka rice market during Japan's Tokugawa Era. *Journal of Futures Markets* 21, 861–874.

Jabir, A., Gupta, K.B., 2011. Efficiency in agricultural commodity futures markets in India: Evidence from cointegration and causality tests. *Agricultural Finance Review* 71, 162–178.

Johansen, S., 1991. Estimation and hypothesis testing of cointegration vectors in gaussian vector autoregressive models. *Econometrica* 59, 1551–1580.

Johansen, S., Juselius, K., 1990. Maximum likelihood estimation and inference on cointegration — With applications to the demand for money. *Oxford Bulletin of Economics and Statistics* 52, 169–210.

Kellard, N., 2002. Evaluating commodity market efficiency: Are cointegration tests appropriate? *Journal of Agricultural Economics* 53, 513–529.

Lai, K.S., Lai, M., 1991. A cointegration test for market efficiency. *Journal of Futures Markets* 11, 567–575.

McKenzie, A.M., Jiang, B., Djunaidi, H., Hoffman, L.A., 2002. Unbiasedness and market efficiency tests of the U.S. rice futures market. *Review of Agricultural Economics* 24, 474–493.

Ministry of Consumer Affairs, Food and Public Distribution (MOCAFPD), various issues. *Annual Report*. MOCAFPD, New Delhi.

Phillips, P.C.B., Hansen, B.E., 1990. Statistical inference in instrumental variables regression with I(1) processes. *Review of Economic Studies* 57, 99–125.

Saikkonen, P., 1992. Estimation and testing of cointegrated systems by an autoregressive approximation. *Econometric Theory* 8, 1–27.

Schaede, U., 1989. Forwards and futures in Tokugawa-period Japan: A new perspective on the Dojima rice market. *Journal of Banking and Finance* 13, 487–513.

Securities and Exchange Board of India (SEBI), 2012. *Handbook of Statistics on the Indian Securities Market 2011.* SEBI, Mumbai.

Stock, J.H., Watson, M.W., 1993. A simple estimator of cointegrating vectors in higher order integrated systems. *Econometrica* 61, 783–820.

Vishwanathan, I., Pillai, A., 2010. Price discovery and convergence in the Indian commodity market. *Indian Growth and Development Review* 3, 53–61.

Wang, H.H., Ke, B., 2005. Efficiency tests of agricultural commodity futures market in China. *Australian Journal of Agricultural and Resource Economics* 49, 125–141.

Xin, Y., Chen, G., Firth, M., 2006. The efficiency of the Chinese commodity futures markets: Development and empirical evidence. *China & World Economy* 14, 79–92.

Chapter 6

What are the Sources of Real and Nominal Exchange Rate Fluctuations? Evidence from SVAR Analysis for India

6.1 Introduction

During the past several decades, India has gone through a transformation of its exchange rate regime. India adopted a fixed exchange regime from 1947 to 1991, and the rupee was pegged to gold until December 1971. The currency was then pegged to the British pound sterling up to September 1975, and thereafter, to a basket of currencies. Subsequently, after a transitional period of dual exchange rates, India shifted to a managed float regime in March 1993. Although the nominal value of the rupee remained stable *vis-à-vis* the US dollar for a while, it has begun to exhibit relatively volatile two-way movements since the mid-1990s.

Figure 6.1 traces the time path of the 36-currency trade-based real and nominal effective exchange rates (FY 1993 $=$ 100) from 1993 to 2008. During this period, the real effective exchange rate (REER) appears to have fluctuated around a constant trend or displayed a tendency to move according to the mean-reversion process during this period; meanwhile, the nominal effective exchange rate (NEER) depreciated until mid-2006, and since then it has displayed a tendency to appreciate. Formally, the Reserve Bank of India (RBI) states that, as the central bank, its primary objective in the foreign exchange market is to manage volatility with no fixed target for the exchange rate, which is determined by market forces. However, empirical studies do not support this official statement and have indicated that the RBI does attempt to maintain the real exchange rate at a fixed target (Kohli, 2003; Jha, 2008).

87

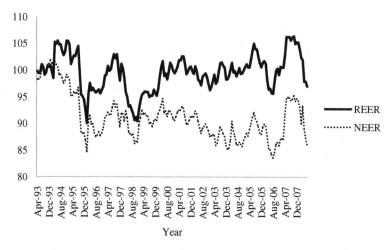

Figure 6.1   The Movements of the Effective Exchange Rates
Source: RBI (2008).

There are several reasons why policymakers in developing countries like India have paid considerable attention to real exchange rate volatility; one of the most important reasons is that the real exchange rate has a substantial impact on export price competitiveness. In April 1997, the Indian government announced that it would achieve a 1% share in world trade by 2002, and in April 2008, it also declared a medium-term target of achieving a 5% share in world trade in both goods and services by 2020. As Srinivasan and Wallack (2003) and Veeramani (2008), among others found, there exists a negative and significant relationship between the real exchange rate and exports in India. Therefore, in the context of external competitiveness, it is worthwhile to investigate the sources of exchange rate fluctuations in India.

There is a growing body of literature that empirically analyzes the sources of exchange rate fluctuations. Examples include Lastrapes (1992), Clarida and Gali (1994), Enders and Lee (1997), Rogers (1999), Chen (2004), and Hamori and Hamori (2007) for industrialized countries, and Dibooglu and Kutan (2001), Chowdhury (2004), and Wang (2005) for less developed countries.

Relevant prior research on India consists of Pattnaik *et al.* (2003) and Moore and Pentecost (2006). Both studies applied a bivariate vector autore-gression (VAR) model of nominal and real exchange rates and examined which real or nominal shocks are main sources of the real exchange rate movements.[1] Both studies employed the restriction of Enders and Lee (1997), which assumes that nominal shocks have a lasting effect on the nominal exchange rate but not on the real exchange rate. Pattnaik *et al.* (2003) used data from the period between April 1993 and December 2001, whereas Moore and Pentecost (2006) used data from the period between March 1993 and January 2004. From their empirical results, both studies concluded that real shocks are the main sources of fluctuations in both nominal and real exchange rates in India.

The purpose of this chapter is to investigate the sources of exchange rate fluctuations in India by applying the structural VAR (SVAR) model. This study differs from prior literature in the following manner. First, we employ the trivariate VAR model including the relative output of India and a foreign country, nominal exchange rate, and real exchange rate between India and a foreign country. Unlike Clarida and Gali (1994) and others, using the nominal exchange rate instead of the relative price level enables an easier comparison of the results with prior studies on India. Second, considering the close trade relations, we alternately use the United States or the euro area as a foreign country in the VAR system; this enables us to confirm the robustness of the empirical results. Finally, this study examines the more recent period of January 1999 to February 2009, whereas previous studies on India examined the period from 1993 to the early 2000s. The sample period in this study corresponds roughly to the period of large capital inflows into India.

The remainder of this chapter is organized in the following manner: Section 6.2 provides the definitions and data sources. Section 6.3 presents a brief explanation of the empirical techniques. Section 6.4 presents the empirical results for India and the United States and for India and the euro area, respectively. Section 6.5 presents the concluding remarks, summarizes the main findings of this study, and provides policy implications.

6.2 Data

The data was obtained from the International Monetary Fund (2009). Our empirical analysis was conducted on the basis of monthly observations

---

[1]Regarding the exchange rate, Pattnaik *et al.* (2003) used India's effective exchange rate, while Moore and Pentecost (2006) used the Indian rupee rate against the US dollar.

during the period from January 1999 to February 2009. We used exchange rates, the consumer price indexes, and the industrial production index (IPI) (seasonally adjusted) for India, the United States, and the euro area. The exchange rate is expressed per unit of the foreign currency (US dollar or euro).

The log of the real exchange rate (re_t), log of the relative output (y_t), and log of the nominal exchange rate (e_t) were used for empirical analysis. The log-level real exchange rate, re_t, can be expressed in the following manner:

$$re_t = e_t + p_t^F - p_t^{Ind}, \tag{1}$$

where p_t^{Ind} is the logarithm of the price level in India and p_t^F is the logarithm of the price level in a foreign country (the United States or the euro area). Thus, the real exchange rate measures the relative price of foreign goods in terms of domestic goods. Moreover, $y_t (= y_t^{Ind} - y_t^F)$ is the difference between the real incomes in India and a foreign country. As a preliminary exercise, the presence of a unit root in the univariate representations of the relative output, real exchange rates, and nominal exchange rates is tested for by using the augmented Dickey–Fuller test (Dickey and Fuller, 1979). For the log-level of each variable, the null hypothesis of a unit root is not rejected at conventional significance level. For the first difference of each variable, the null hypothesis of a unit root is rejected at the conventional significance level. Thus, all variables are found to be $I(1)$ series.

6.3 Empirical Technique

We use the trivariate system for empirical analysis given by,

$$x_t = [y_t, re_t, e_t]'. \tag{2}$$

Let us consider the following infinite-order vector moving average (VMA) representation:

$$\Delta x_t = C(L)\varepsilon_t, \tag{3}$$

where L is a lag operator, Δ is a difference operator, and $\varepsilon_t = [\varepsilon_{s,t}, \varepsilon_{d,t}, \varepsilon_{n,t}]'$ is a (3×1) vector for the covariance matrix of structural shocks Σ.

The error terms can be interpreted as the relative supply shocks, relative real demand shocks, and relative nominal shocks. We assume that structural shocks have no contemporaneous correlation or autocorrelation. This implies that Σ is a diagonal matrix.

Further, to implement the econometric methodology, it is necessary to estimate the following finite-order VAR model:

$$[I - \Phi(L)]\Delta x_t = u_t, \tag{4}$$

where $\Phi(L)$ is a finite-order matrix polynomial in the lag operator and u_t is a vector of disturbances. If the stationarity condition is satisfied, Equation (3) can be transferred to the VMA representation:

$$\Delta x_t = A(L)u_t, \tag{5}$$

where $A(L)$ is a lag polynomial. Equations (3) and (5) imply a linear relationship between ε_t and u_t in the following manner:

$$u_t = C_0 \varepsilon_t. \tag{6}$$

In Equation (6), C_0 is a 3×3 matrix that defines the contemporaneous structural relationship among the three variables. Moreover, it is necessary to identify the vector of structural shocks, so that it can be recovered from the estimated disturbance vector. We require nine parameters to convert the residuals from the estimated VAR into the original shocks that drive the behavior of the endogenous variables. Since six of these nine parameters are given by the elements of $\sum = C_0 C_0'$, three more identifying restrictions need to be added. According to Blanchard and Quah (1989), economic theory can be used to impose these restrictions. Thus, using the methodology given by Clarida and Gali (1994), we impose the following three additional restrictions on the long-run multipliers, while freely determining the short-run dynamics.

(i) Nominal (monetary) shocks have no long-run impact on the levels of output.

(ii) Nominal (monetary) shocks have no long-run impact on the real exchange rate.

(iii) Real demand shocks have no long-run impact on the levels of output.

The long-run representation of Equation (3) can be written as

$$
\begin{bmatrix} \Delta y_t \\ \Delta re_t \\ \Delta e_t \end{bmatrix} = \begin{bmatrix} C_{11}(1) & C_{12}(1) & C_{13}(1) \\ C_{21}(1) & C_{22}(1) & C_{23}(1) \\ C_{31}(1) & C_{32}(1) & C_{33}(1) \end{bmatrix} \begin{bmatrix} \varepsilon_{s,t} \\ \varepsilon_{d,t} \\ \varepsilon_{n,t} \end{bmatrix},
\tag{7}
$$

where $C(1) = C_0 + C_1 + C_2 + \cdots$ are long-run multipliers in our SVAR model (long-run effect of Δx_t). Following the methodology of Clarida and Gali (1994), we stipulate that the long-run multipliers C_{12}, C_{13}, and C_{23} are equal to zero, thereby making the matrix a lower triangular matrix.

However, our analysis differs from the analyses of Clarida and Gali (1994). Our system comprises the relative output level, real exchange rate, and nominal exchange rate, while their system comprises the relative output level, real exchange rate, and relative price level. By using the nominal exchange rate instead of the relative price level, we focus on the effect of various shocks on both real and nominal exchange rates.

In the empirical analysis, using the Akaike Information Criterion (AIC) developed by Akaike (1974) and Schwarz Bayesian Information Criterion (SBIC) developed by Schwarz (1978) to choose the optimal lag length of VAR, we find that the VAR (1) model is the most appropriate for the system. To shed light on the sources of each variable, we calculate the forecast error variance decomposition. Variance decomposition is a convenient measure of the relative importance of such shocks with respect to the overall system.

6.4 Empirical Results

6.4.1 Results for India and the United States

We begin with the case of India and the United States. Table 6.1 presents the results of the forecast error variance for real and nominal exchange rates that can be attributed to each shock at different horizons in the system. Throughout the time horizons, real demand shocks — the most important factor in the variation in the forecast error of the real exchange rate — account for more than 97% of the variance in the real exchange rate. The remaining variance is attributed to real supply and nominal shocks. Meanwhile, real supply shocks account for less than 1% of the forecast error variance in the real exchange rate. Nominal shocks account for approximately 2% of the variation in the forecast error of real exchange rate. In other words, real

Table 6.1   Forecast Error Variance Decomposition (India and the United States)

Horizon (months)	Real Supply Shocks (%)	Real Demand Shocks (%)	Nominal Shocks (%)
(a) Real Exchange Rate			
1	0.561	97.566	1.873
3	0.727	97.171	2.102
6	0.736	97.089	2.175
9	0.736	97.087	2.177
12	0.736	97.087	2.177
18	0.736	97.087	2.177
24	0.736	97.087	2.177
36	0.736	97.087	2.177
(b) Nominal Exchange Rate			
1	0.007	84.965	15.028
3	1.174	79.543	19.282
6	1.255	79.120	19.625
9	1.256	79.114	19.630
12	1.256	79.113	19.630
18	1.256	79.113	19.630
24	1.256	79.113	19.630
36	1.256	79.113	19.630

demand shocks are responsible for most of the forecast error variance of the movement in the real exchange rate.

Further, forecast error variance decomposition for the variation in nominal exchange rates suggests that real demand shocks explain most nominal exchange rate movements as well. Real demand shocks, which are the most important factor, account for approximately 79% of the variation in nominal exchange rate movements. Meanwhile, nominal shocks account for approximately 20% of the forecast error variance. On the other hand, real supply shocks account for less than 1.3% of nominal exchange rate fluctuations.

To summarize, real demand shocks are the source of a substantial share of the forecast error variance of real and nominal exchange rate movements between India and the United States. The significance of real shocks in explaining real and nominal exchange rate movements is consistent with the evidence presented by Pattnaik *et al.* (2003) and Moore and Pentecost

Table 6.2   Forecast Error Variance Decomposition (India and the Euro Area)

Horizon (months)	Real Supply Shocks (%)	Real Demand Shocks (%)	Nominal Shocks (%)
(a) Real Exchange Rate			
1	1.522	97.746	0.732
3	2.003	96.940	1.056
6	2.022	96.918	1.060
9	2.023	96.918	1.060
12	2.023	96.918	1.060
18	2.023	96.918	1.060
24	2.023	96.918	1.060
36	2.023	96.918	1.060
(b) Nominal Exchange Rate			
1	0.553	95.145	4.302
3	1.430	93.205	5.364
6	1.467	93.162	5.371
9	1.468	93.161	5.371
12	1.468	93.161	5.371
18	1.468	93.161	5.371
24	1.468	93.161	5.371
36	1.468	93.161	5.371

(2006) for India as well as studies such as Lastrapes (1992), Enders and Lee (1997), and Chowdhury (2004) for other countries.

6.4.2   Results for India and the euro area

Here, we analyze the case of India and the euro area. Using the AIC and SBIC, we again find that the VAR (1) model is the most appropriate for the system. The results of forecast error variance decomposition are reported in Table 6.2.

Variance decompositions in the real exchange rate suggest that real demand shocks explain most of the movement in the real exchange rate. Real demand shocks, which are the most important factor, account for more than 96% of the real exchange rate variation. Meanwhile, real supply shocks explain approximately 2% of the forecast error variance. Nominal shocks account for approximately 1% of the real exchange rate movements.

To summarize, real demand shocks account for most of the forecast error variance of the movement in the real exchange rate.

Further, forecast error variance decompositions for nominal exchange rates indicate that real demand shocks are responsible for approximately 93% of the variation in the changes of nominal exchange rates. Real supply shocks account for approximately 1.5% of the variation in nominal exchange rates and nominal shocks account for approximately 5.4% of the variation in nominal exchange rate movements.

To summarize, real demand shocks are the source of a substantial share of the forecast error variance of the real and nominal exchange rate movements between India and the euro area. These empirical results for the euro area are consistent with those for the United States.

6.5 Concluding Remarks

Some empirical studies have stated that the RBI has managed to target the real exchange rate in India. The time path of REER seems to support this result, although the RBI itself has not formally acknowledged it. In addition, there are some recommendations that the Indian central bank should maintain the real exchange rate at a constant level. For example, the Committee on Fuller Capital Convertibility repeatedly recommended to the RBI that it should monitor the exchange rate within a band of $\pm 0.5\%$ around the neutral REER and that it should ordinarily intervene when the REER moves beyond this band (RBI, 2006).

This study analyzed the sources of exchange rate fluctuations in India from 1999 to 2009. We employed the trivariate VAR model in the analysis, which comprises the relative output of India and a foreign country and the nominal and real exchange rates between India and a foreign country. The results demonstrated that real shocks have a persistent effect on both real and nominal exchange rate movements, which is consistent with relevant literature. Moreover, we observed that real demand shocks play a key role among real shocks. These results were obtained by using either the United States or the euro area as a foreign country; thus, they were robust in this sense.

The results of this study suggest that the RBI should not attempt to target the real exchange rate over time. Since real shocks are the dominant explanation for real exchange rate fluctuations, it is impractical for the RBI to attempt to maintain the real exchange rate at a predetermined level in the long run, although there is some room for monetary and exchange rate policies to manage real exchange rate fluctuations in the short to medium term. Consequently, based on these results, we conclude that the RBI cannot influence international competitiveness through its exchange rate policy; in order to improve international competitiveness, policymakers should focus on the real side of the economy, such as the improvement of efficiency, technologies, and productivity in the Indian economy.

References

Akaike, H., 1974. A new look at the statistical model identification. *IEEE Transactions on Automatic Control* AC-19, 716–723.

Blanchard, O., Quah, D., 1989. The dynamic effects of aggregate demand and supply disturbances. *American Economic Review* 79, 655–673.

Chen, S.S., 2004. Real exchange rate fluctuations and monetary shocks: A revisit. *International Journal of Finance & Economics* 9, 25–32.

Chowdhury, I.S., 2004. Sources of exchange rate fluctuations: Empirical evidence from six emerging market countries. *Applied Financial Economics* 14, 697–705.

Clarida, R., Gali, J., 1994. Sources of real exchange rate fluctuations: How important are nominal shocks? NBER Working Paper Series 4658, The National Bureau of Economic Research, Cambridge, MA.

Dibooglu, S., Kutan, A.M., 2001. Sources of real exchange rate fluctuations in transition economies: The case of Poland and Hungary. *Journal of Comparative Economics* 29, 257–275.

Dickey, D.A., Fuller, W.A., 1979. Distribution of the estimators for autoregressive time series with a unit root. *Journal of the American Statistical Association* 74, 427–431.

Enders, W., Lee, B.S., 1997. Accounting for real and nominal exchange rate movements in the post-Bretton Woods period. *Journal of International Money and Finance* 16, 233–254.

Hamori, S., Hamori, N., 2007. Sources of real and nominal exchange rate movements for the Euro. *Economics Bulletin* 6, 1–10.

International Monetary Fund (IMF), 2009. *International Financial Statistics, July*. IMF, Washington, DC.

Jha, R., 2008. Inflation targeting in India: Issues and prospects. *International Review of Applied Economics* 22, 259–270.

Kohli, R., 2003. Real exchange rate stabilisation and managed floating: Exchange rate policy in India, 1993–2001. *Journal of Asian Economics* 14, 369–387.

Lastrapes, W.D., 1992. Sources of fluctuations in real and nominal exchange rates. *The Review of Economics and Statistics* 74, 530–539.

Moore, T., Pentecost, E.J., 2006. The sources of real exchange rate fluctuations in India. *Indian Economic Review* 41, 9–23.

Pattnaik, R.K., Kapur, M., Dhal, S.C., 2003. Exchange rate policy and management: The Indian experience. *Economic and Political Weekly* 38, 2139–2154.

Reserve Bank of India (RBI), 2006. *Report of the Committee on Fuller Capital Account Convertibility*. RBI, Mumbai.

Reserve Bank of India (RBI), 2008. *Handbook of Statistics on Indian Economy 2007–08*. RBI, Mumbai.

Rogers, J.H., 1999. Monetary shocks and real exchange rates. *Journal of International Economics* 49, 269–288.

Schwarz, G., 1978. Estimating the dimension of a model. *The Annals of Statistics* 6, 461–464.

Srinivasan, T.N., Wallack, J., 2003. Export performance and the real effective exchange rate, in: Krueger, A.O., Chinoy, S.Z. (Eds.), *Reforming India's External, Financial, and Fiscal Policies*. Stanford University Press, Stanford, pp. 51–54.

Veeramani, C., 2008. Impact of exchange rate appreciation on India's exports. *Economic and Political Weekly* 43, 10–14.

Wang, T., 2005. Sources of real exchange rate fluctuations in China. *Journal of Comparative Economics* 33, 753–771.

Part 3

**Financial Development and
Poverty Alleviation in India**

Chapter 7

How Has Financial Deepening Affected
Poverty Reduction in India?

7.1 Introduction

Financial development is considered to be an integral factor in the economic growth of a country. Many studies have noted that a well-functioning financial system that mobilizes savings, allocates resources, and facilitates risk management contributes to economic growth by supporting capital accumulation, improving investment efficiency, and promoting technological innovation (Kirkpatrick, 2000, p. 366). It has also been argued that economic growth creates demand for financial services, which in turn leads to financial development. Indeed, cross-country studies, such as King and Levine (1993a), Demirgüç-Kunt and Maksimovic (1996), Levine and Zervos (1998), among others, find that higher levels of financial development are significantly and robustly associated with faster rates of economic growth (Bhattacharya and Sivasubramanian, 2003, p. 905). Moreover, empirical studies employing a causality method suggest that there may be a bidirectional causal relationship between financial development and economic growth (e.g., Demetriades and Hussein, 1996; Luintel and Khan, 1999; Apergis et al., 2007).

However, this close relationship between finance and growth do not necessarily mean that financial development contributes to poverty reduction (Beck et al., 2007, p. 46). Typically, governments in developing countries face the task of achieving economic growth with equitable income distribution and poverty reduction. In other words, economic growth can be categorized as either growth with rising income inequality and poverty or growth with falling income inequality and poverty. The differences between these two categories can alter the impacts of growth on the poor. If financial development increases average growth by increasing the incomes of only the rich, and hence worsening income inequality, then financial development will not help the poor (*ibid.*, p. 46). Therefore, based on the close relationship between finance and growth, a growing body of empirical studies has analyzed the effects of financial deepening on income distribution on the one hand and poverty conditions on the other.

Studies on financial deepening and income distribution, such as Li *et al.* (1998), Milanovic (2005), Clarke *et al.* (2006), Beck *et al.* (2007), Kai and Hamori (2009), and Ang (2010), generally observe that financial deepening helps reduce income inequality. Most studies on financial deepening and poverty (e.g., Honohan, 2004; Jalilian and Kirkpatrick, 2005; Beck *et al.*, 2007; Jeanneney and Kpodar, 2008; Quartey, 2008; Odhiambo, 2009, 2010) point out that financial deepening affects poverty reduction not only directly but also indirectly, through its impact on economic growth. In short, prior research tends to suggest that financial deepening contributes to both inequality reduction and poverty alleviation. However, these findings are mostly based on data for a large sample of countries; in this study, we examine whether the findings from previous studies can be applied to a specific country, India.

We chose to examine poverty issues in India because the country is estimated to include the world's largest number of poor people. Over the last few decades, the poverty ratio in India has steadily decreased. In fact, according to national estimates, the percentage of the population below the poverty line (poverty headcount ratio) has fallen from 54.9% in FY 1973 to 27.5% in FY 2004. During the same period, however, the number of people below the poverty line decreased only slightly, from 321 million to 317 million, partly because of rapid growth of the national population. Recently, under the slogan of "inclusive growth", the Indian government has been targeting poverty reduction through economic growth, accompanied by equitable distribution of the benefits of growth among all people, including those in the poor and weaker sections of society. Meanwhile, Chen and Ravallion (2008) point out that, in India, around 456 million people still live below the new international poverty line of USD 1.25 a day, based on 2005 purchasing power parity prices. This corresponds to one-third of the world's poor, and exceeds the number of poor in sub-Saharan Africa as a whole. Therefore, although India has enjoyed rapid economic growth for a decade, poverty reduction remains one of its biggest challenges.

In this chapter, we empirically analyze the poverty issue in India, focusing especially on the poverty reduction effect of financial deepening. This study follows Ang's (2010) recent finding, in the course of an investigation into the impact of financial deepening on income distribution that, financial development helps reduce income inequality in India.[1] In our empirical analysis, we consider models in which the poverty headcount ratios for the whole economy, as well as for urban and rural areas separately, are explained by financial-deepening and control variables, including economic growth, international openness, and the inflation rate. We then estimate the models by using unbalanced panel data on 28 states and union territories for seven time periods between FY 1973 and FY 2004. Empirical results mainly indicate the following. First, the coefficients of financial deepening are estimated to have a significant negative value, suggesting that an increase in financial development helps to alleviate poverty in India. Second, economic growth also displays a significant positive effect on poverty alleviation. Third, the coefficients of international openness are estimated to have a significant positive value, suggesting that greater international openness has the effect of increasing poverty. Fourth, similar to international openness, a rising inflation rate has an adverse effect on poverty alleviation. These findings are robust to changes in the dependent variable, namely, the poverty ratio in rural areas, urban areas, or the economy as a whole.

The chapter is organized as follows. Section 7.2 briefly reviews relevant literature and discusses the contributions of this study. Section 7.3 explains the definitions, sources, and properties of the data, and Section 7.4 presents the models. In Section 7.5, we show the empirical results, and the final section summarizes the main findings of this study and suggests policy implications.

---

[1]Ang (2010) states that, in India, financial deepening appears to have a different effect on income inequality than financial liberalization. He empirically analyzes how income inequality responds to financial sector reforms by using various measures of financial liberalization and finds that, unlike financial deepening, financial liberalization seems to have a harmful effect on income distribution.

7.2 Literature Review

Recently, there has been an increasing number of empirical analyses of large samples of countries about the effects of financial deepening on poverty reduction — Honohan (2004), Jalilian and Kirkpatrick (2005), Beck *et al.* (2007), and Jeanneney and Kpodar (2008), to cite a few.[2] For example, Honohan (2004) attempted to explore the association between financial depth, as measured by private credit, and the poverty ratio, using cross-country data available for more than 70 developing countries. He found that financial depth is negatively associated with the poverty ratio, even after controlling for the mean income, the income share of the top 10%, and the inflation rate.

Jalilian and Kirkpatrick (2005) also examined whether financial sector development can contribute to the goal of poverty reduction in many developed and developing countries, including India. In analyzing this relationship, they incorporate three distinct research strands, linking financial development to economic growth, economic growth to poverty, and financial development to inequality. Estimating each link separately, they found that the ratio of private credit to gross domestic product (GDP), a proxy for financial development, improves growth prospects, especially in poorer developing countries; that the income of the poor changes along with average income; and that financial development has an inverted U-shaped relationship with income inequality. Based on this evidence, Jalilian and Kirkpatrick (2005, p. 652) concluded that financial development helps reduce poverty; their results indicate that a unit change in financial development improves income growth prospects of the poor by almost 0.3%.

Beck *et al.* (2007) estimated changes in both income distribution and poverty levels relative to financial development in order to investigate its impact on the poor because financial development may affect both aggregate growth and income distribution. Specifically, they regressed the dependent variables — increases in the Gini coefficient, income share of the lowest quintile, and poverty ratio — on the private credit to GDP ratio, a proxy for financial development, based on panel data for 72 countries from 1960

---

[2]Jalilian and Kirkpatrick (2002) and Beck *et al.* (2004) also analyzed the impact of financial development on poverty reduction, using a large sample of countries. They drew similar conclusions to those of Jalilian and Kirkpatrick (2005) and Beck *et al.* (2007).

to 2005 (68 countries from 1980 to 2005 for poverty ratio growth). They found that an increase in financial development lowers income inequality, increases disproportionately the income of the relatively poor, and is strongly associated with poverty alleviation.

Moreover, Jeanneney and Kpodar (2008) assessed how financial development helps reduce poverty, not only directly but also indirectly through economic growth. Using panel data for 75 developing countries from 1966 through 1999, they employed the generalized method of moments (GMM) system to estimate models in which the average per capita income of the poorest 20% of the population is explained by real GDP per capita, the level and instability of financial development, and a set of control variables. Financial development is measured by either M3/GDP or private credit/GDP, whereas financial instability is defined as the average absolute value of residuals, obtained by regressing the indicator of financial development on its lagged value and a linear trend. Their results indicated that financial development measured by M3/GDP has a significant positive relationship with the mean income of the poor, that the direct effect of financial development on poverty reduction is greater than the indirect effect through economic growth, and that financial instability associated with financial development significantly reduces the income of the poor, partially offsetting the benefits of financial development.

As with the studies referred to above, prior empirical studies based on large samples of countries generally suggest that financial deepening and economic growth are effective in alleviating poverty. There have also been studies on the relationship between finance and poverty within particular countries. For example, Quartey (2008) and Odhiambo (2009, 2010), each focusing on a sub-Saharan African country, examined the causal relationship between financial deepening and poverty reduction within each country by applying the Granger causality test and the cointegration test.

Quartey (2008) explored the interrelationship between financial development, savings mobilization, and poverty reduction in Ghana from 1970 to 2001. Conducting a pairwise causality test, he found that financial development, measured as the ratio of private credit to GDP, Granger-causes poverty reduction, measured in terms of per capita consumption, although it does not Granger-cause savings mobilization. Odhiambo (2009) examined the dynamic relationships among financial development, economic growth, and poverty reduction in South Africa from 1960 to 2006, employing a trivariate causality test based on an error correction model. The empirical results of the Granger causality test indicated that M2/GDP (a proxy for financial development) and economic growth cause an increase in per capita consumption (a proxy for poverty reduction), and that economic growth leads to financial development. Moreover, Odhiambo (2010) empirically analyzed the causal relationship between financial development and poverty alleviation in Zambia from 1969 to 2006. She examined the effect of three financial development proxies — M2/GDP, private credit/GDP, and domestic money bank assets — on per capita consumption, a proxy for poverty levels. Using a bivariate causality test based on an error correction model, she found that financial development seems to cause poverty reduction when private credit and domestic money bank assets are used, while the reverse causality is found when M2/GDP is used. Table 7.1 summarizes the above-mentioned literature on the finance-poverty nexus.

This study differs from the reviewed literature as follows. First, we examine the impact of financial deepening on poverty alleviation in India utilizing state-wise panel data. As far as we are aware, this is the first attempt to analyze the finance-poverty nexus in India using a state-level framework. Second, in estimating the models, we apply the dynamic GMM estimator to panel data. This allows us to examine the dynamic movement of dependent variables and to deal with the endogeneity problem. Third, in contrast to prior studies that use private credit and/or monetary aggregates as proxy variables for financial development, this study utilizes the amount of credit and deposits of the scheduled commercial banks to measure financial depth in India.[3] This reflects the relatively important role of

---

[3] In India, commercial banks can be broadly classified into two categories: scheduled and non-scheduled banks. Scheduled banks are the banks included in the Second Schedule of the Reserve Bank of India Act. Scheduled banks are entitled to certain privileges from the central bank, such as refinancing, loans and advances, and authorized dealer's licenses to handle foreign exchange business (RBI, 1995, p. 108). Correspondingly, scheduled banks are required to maintain a minimum amount of capital and obey the central bank directives on cash reserves (Sen and Vaidya, 1997, p. 37). In contrast, non-scheduled banks are excluded from the Second Schedule of the Reserve Bank of India Act. In fact, almost all of the commercial banks in India are classified as scheduled banks.

Table 7.1   Summary of Literature on the Finance-Poverty Nexus

Study	1) Period 2) Region/Country	Financial Deepening Measure	Poverty Measure	Main Findings
Honohan (2004)	1) — 2) 70 to 76 countries	Private credit/GDP	Poverty headcount ratio	Financial depth is negatively associated with headcount poverty, even after taking account of mean income and inequality.
Jalilian and Kirkpatrick (2005)	1) 1960–1995 2) 42 countries	Private credit/GDP	Growth of income of the poor	Financial sector growth contributes to poverty reduction through the growth enhancing effect, up to a threshold level of economic development.
Beck *et al.* (2007)	1) 1980–2005 2) 68 countries	Private credit/GDP	Growth of poverty headcount ratio	Financial development is associated with poverty alleviation.
Jeanneney and Kpodar (2008)	1) 1966–1999 2) 75 countries	Private credit/GDP or M3/GDP	Average per capita income of the poor (or poverty headcount ratio/ poverty gap)	Financial development measured by M3/GDP has a significant positive relationship with the mean income of the poor.
Quartey (2008)	1) 1970–2001 2) Ghana	Private credit/GDP or M2/GDP	Per capita consumption	Financial sector development measured by private credit/GDP Granger-causes poverty reduction.
Odhiambo (2009)	1) 1960–2006 2) South Africa	M2/GDP	Per capita consumption	Both financial development and economic growth Granger-causes poverty reduction, while economic growth Granger-causes financial development.
Odhiambo (2010)	1) 1969–2006 2) Zambia	Private credit/GDP, M2/GDP, or domestic money bank assets	Per capita consumption	Financial development causes poverty reduction when private credit/GDP or domestic money bank assets are used, while the reverse causality is detected when M2/GDP is used.

commercial banks in the Indian financial system. Fourth, in our empirical analysis of finance and poverty, we consider economic growth, international openness, and the inflation rate as control variables. To measure the degree of international openness, we use two indicators: openness to trade and foreign investment. Finally, in this study, we present empirical results for the economy as a whole and for rural and urban areas separately, as well as the impact of individual explanatory variables on the poverty ratio in each area.

7.3 Data

To assess the impact of financial development on poverty, this study uses unbalanced panel data of 28 states and union territories in India for seven selected years from FY 1973 to FY 2004 (1973, 1977, 1983, 1987, 1993, 1999, and 2004).[4,5] The poverty ratio is the explained variable, while financial deepening and other conditioning information variables are the explanatory variables (see Table 7.2 for more precise definitions).

The poverty headcount ratio (*POV*) is measured by the state-wise poverty ratio, namely, the percentage of people below the poverty line set by the Indian government.[6] We consider the *POV* for the country as a whole as well as separately for urban and rural areas. The data are obtained from

---

[4]The 28 states and union territories covered in this study are as follows: Andhra Pradesh, Arunachal Pradesh, Assam, Bihar, Goa, Gujarat, Haryana, Himachal Pradesh, Jammu & Kashmir, Karnataka, Kerala, Madhya Pradesh, Maharashtra, Manipur, Meghalaya, Mizoram, Nagaland, Odisha, Punjab, Rajasthan, Sikkim, Tamil Nadu, Tripura, West Bengal, Andaman & Nicobar Islands, Chandigarh, Delhi, and Puducherry.

[5]All benchmark years are fiscal years except for 1983, which is the calendar year.

[6]In India, the poverty line is based on a minimum consumption expenditure anchored to a nutritional norm of 2,400 calories per person per day in rural areas and 2,100 calories per person per day in urban areas (RBI, 2009, p. 494). These poverty lines are then applied to the household consumption expenditure distribution of the National Sample Survey Organization (NSSO) to estimate the proportion and number of poor at the state level (*ibid.*, p. 494). Although the 61st round of the Consumer Expenditure Survey conducted in FY 2004 by the NSSO permits comparable estimates of inequality and poverty with the 50th (FY 1993) and earlier rounds, it is not strictly comparable to the 55th round (FY 1999) because the design of the National Sample Survey changed in the 55th round (Datt and Ravallion, 2002, pp. 93–94; Himanshu, 2007, p. 497).

Table 7.2   Definition and Sources of Each Variable

Variables	Definition	Sources
POV	The percentage of the population below the poverty line (poverty headcount ratio) of each region	RBI (2009) and the Web sites of the Planning Commission (http://planningcommission.gov.in/) and Indiastat.com (http://www.indiastat.com/default.aspx)
*FD*1	logarithm of credit amount in a state as a share of the regional output in the same region	Various issues of Banking Statistics and Basic Statistical Returns of Scheduled Commercial Banks in India published by the RBI (Regional output (Net State Domestic Product: NSDP) from the Web sites of the Ministry of Statistics and Programme Implementation (MOSPI) (http://mospi.nic.in/Mospi_New/site/home.aspx) and Indiastat.com (http://www.indiastat.com/default.aspx))
*FD*2	logarithm of deposit amount in a state as a share of the regional output in the same region	
*OPEN*1	Ratio of exports plus imports to nominal GDP	RBI (2009)
*OPEN*2	Ratio of the net inflow of foreign direct investment to nominal GDP	World Bank (2008) (Nominal GDP from RBI (2009))
INF	The log difference of the WPI	RBI (2009)
y	The growth rate of per capita NSDP	The Web sites of the MOSPI (http://mospi.nic.in/Mospi_New/site/home.aspx) and Indiastat.com (http://www.indiastat.com/default.aspx)

the Reserve Bank of India (RBI) (2009), and the Web sites of the Planning Commission and Indiastat.com.

Financial deepening is measured by two variables: the logarithm of a region's scheduled commercial bank credit (*FD*1) and deposits (*FD*2) as ratios to the output of the region. Each measure is related to the scheduled commercial banks since they have played a dominant role in the Indian financial system; they have typically accounted for around 70% of the total assets of financial intermediaries in India, at least during the last couple of decades.

Financial deepening is thought to promote efficient credit allocation, reduce risk through diversified investment in financial intermediaries, and lower the transaction costs of these intermediaries through information generation. Therefore, it is generally believed that financial deepening will promote economic growth and, in turn, reduce income inequality. Furthermore, financial deepening can be regarded as a contributory factor in poverty reduction by eliminating credit constraints on the poor and increasing their productive assets and productivity (World Bank, 2001; Jalilian and Kirkpatrick, 2002). As stated in the previous section, empirical analyses, albeit limited, actually support the argument that financial deepening is conducive to poverty reduction.

In terms of the conditioning information, we control for two sets of factors: macroeconomic and regional environments. For the macroeconomic environment, we consider international openness and the inflation rate. For the regional environment, we take into account the output growth rate of each region.

(a) *International openness*

There have been many theoretical and empirical studies conducted to analyze the impact of international openness on the poor in developing countries, but a general consensus on this topic has not yet been achieved. For example, according to the standard general equilibrium trade model, global economic integration should help the poor in developing countries since these countries have a comparative advantage in producing goods that use unskilled labor (Harrison and McMillan, 2007, p. 123). Moreover, empirical studies such as Dollar and Kraay (2004) observe that international openness, measured in terms of trade integration, has the effect of alleviating poverty in a large sample of countries. However, a question is also raised from theoretical and empirical perspectives whether international openness or globalization actually contributes to poverty reduction in developing countries (e.g., Wade, 2004; Milanovic, 2005; Topalova, 2005; Davis and Mishra, 2007). Therefore, this topic requires a more detailed investigation, including country-level analyses.

In this study, we use two variables to capture the degree of international openness in India and its impact on the poverty ratio: the country's exports and imports (*OPEN*1) and the net inflow of foreign direct investment (*OPEN*2) as ratios to the country's GDP. Since the net inflow of foreign direct investment can be negative, we do not use logarithms to measure international openness.

(b) *Inflation rate*

To capture the macroeconomic environment, we also control for India's inflation rate (*INF*). The inflation rate is calculated as the growth rate of the wholesale price index (WPI), obtained from RBI (2009). High and unpredictable inflation is thought to have a disproportionally negative impact on the poor because they have relatively limited access to financial instruments that hedge against inflation and are also likely to have a larger share of cash in their small portfolios (Easterly and Fischer, 2001, p. 160; Holden and Prokopenko, 2001, p. 30). Indeed, prior empirical studies such as Romer and Romer (1998) and Easterly and Fischer (2001) generally support this position for a large sample of countries. Therefore, even in the Indian context, we expect inflation to be detrimental to the poor.

(c) *Output growth*

A large number of studies have pointed out that financial development helps reduce poverty indirectly through its effect on economic growth. This suggests that economic growth is an effective instrument for poverty reduction. However, economic growth may not be a sufficient condition for poverty alleviation (Holden and Prokopenko, 2001, p. 7). Theoretically, it is possible that in certain countries the benefits of economic growth for the poor are undermined or even offset by an increase in income inequality (Jeanneney and Kpodar, 2008, p. 3). However, recent empirical evidence does not support the argument that, in general, economic growth affects income distribution. For example, by using data from a sample of 92 countries over four decades, Dollar and Kraay (2002) empirically find that incomes of the poor on average rise in proportion to average incomes, suggesting that economic growth typically benefits the poor as much as everyone else. Moreover, for 49 developed and developing countries during the period 1947 to 1994, Li *et al.* (1998) observe that income inequality, measured by the Gini coefficient, is relatively stable over time within countries, though it varies significantly across countries. Therefore, based on these research results, economic growth is expected to help alleviate poverty.

To control for economic growth in a regional environment, we use the output growth (y) of a region, calculated as the growth rate of the per capita output in each state and union territory.[7]

7.4 Models

This study uses four models, specified as follows:

Model 1:

$$POV_{it} = \lambda POV_{i,t-1} + \beta_{i0} + \beta_{i1} FD1_{it} + \beta_{i2} OPEN1_t$$
$$+ \beta_{i3} INF_t + \beta_{i4} y_{it} + u_{it}, \tag{1}$$

Model 2:

$$POV_{it} = \lambda POV_{i,t-1} + \beta_{i0} + \beta_{i1} FD1_{it} + \beta_{i2} OPEN2_t$$
$$+ \beta_{i3} INF_t + \beta_{i4} y_{it} + u_{it}, \tag{2}$$

Model 3:

$$POV_{it} = \lambda POV_{i,t-1} + \beta_{i0} + \beta_{i1} FD2_{it} + \beta_{i2} OPEN1_t$$
$$+ \beta_{i3} INF_t + \beta_{i4} y_{it} + u_{it}, \tag{3}$$

Model 4:

$$POV_{it} = \lambda POV_{i,t-1} + \beta_{i0} + \beta_{i1} FD2_{it} + \beta_{i2} OPEN2_t$$
$$+ \beta_{i3} INF_t + \beta_{i4} y_{it} + u_{it}, \tag{4}$$

where POV_{it} is the poverty ratio for region i at time t, $FD1_{it}$ and $FD2_{it}$ are the logarithms of scheduled commercial bank credit and deposit ratios, respectively, to the output of region i at time t, $OPEN1_t$ is the ratio of the country's exports and imports to its GDP at time t, $OPEN2_t$ is the ratio of the net inflow of foreign direct investment into the country to its GDP at time t, INF_t is the country's inflation rate at time t, y_{it} is the growth rate of the per capita output of region i at time t, u_{it} is the error term, $i(= 1, 2, \ldots, N)$ is

---

[7]We also tried using per capita income instead of the growth rate in our empirical analysis. However, we found that the model specification is rejected in most cases when we per capita income is used.

the number of cross-sections, and $t(= 1, 2, \ldots, T)$ is the number of time series.

These models are used to examine the effects of financial deepening on the poverty ratio. Models 1 and 2 employ the ratio of credit to GDP, whereas Models 3 and 4 use the ratio of deposits to GDP, as the measure of financial deepening. Models 1 and 3 utilize the trade to GDP ratio as the degree of international openness, whereas Models 2 and 4 use the foreign direct investment to GDP ratio as the measure of globalization. These models are applied to check whether the empirical results are robust to the choice of financial deepening and international openness measures. We expect that financial development will ease credit constraints on the poor, thus decreasing the poverty ratio. Our analysis uses the inflation rate and the regional growth rate as additional control variables.

7.5 Empirical Results

7.5.1 Results for the whole country

Table 7.3 reports the empirical results of Models 1, 2, 3, and 4 when we use the poverty ratio for the whole country. Since the explanatory variables include the lagged value of the explained variable, we cannot apply the ordinary regression techniques. Instead, we estimate each model using the dynamic panel GMM estimators developed by Arellano and Bond (1991), so that we can also deal with the endogeneity problem.[8]

As is clear from Table 7.3, the coefficients of the credit to regional output ratio (*FD1*) are estimated to be negative (-9.166 for Model 1 and -9.081 for Model 2) and are statistically significant at the 1% level. The empirical results indicate that the coefficients of the deposits to regional output ratio (*FD2*) are estimated to be negative (-11.356 for Model 3 and -11.359 for Model 4) and are statistically significant at the 1% level. Our results reveal that the poverty ratio decreases as the financial system deepens.

With regard to other control variables, we examine the effects of two macro variables on the poverty ratio: the degree of openness and the inflation

---

[8]For each model, the poverty ratio is used as the dynamic instrumental variable, while the openness measure, inflation rate, and regional growth rates are used as the standard instrumental variables.

Indian Economy

Table 7.3   Financial Deepening and Poverty: Whole Country

	Model 1	Model 2	Model 3	Model 4
POV(−1)	−0.223	−0.258	−0.438	−0.488
	(0.001)***	(0.000)***	(0.000)***	(0.000)***
FD1	−9.166	−9.081		
	(0.000)***	(0.000)***		
FD2			−11.356	−11.359
			(0.000)***	(0.000)***
OPEN1	0.002		0.003	
	(0.000)***		(0.000)***	
OPEN2		0.039		0.055
		(0.014)**		(0.033)**
INF	0.327	0.394	0.440	0.535
	(0.000)***	(0.000)***	(0.000)***	(0.000)***
y	−0.997	−0.968	−1.581	−1.543
	(0.000)***	(0.000)***	(0.000)***	(0.000)***
J-statistic	21.286	21.485	20.837	20.812
	(0.067)	(0.064)	(0.076)	(0.077)
Number of Observations	124	124	124	124

Notes: (1) Numbers in parentheses are *p*-values.
(2) Significance at the 1% and 5% level is indicated by *** and **, respectively.
(3) The dependent variable is the poverty ratio (*POV*). *FD*1 is equal to the logarithm of the ratio of scheduled commercial bank credit to the output in a region. *FD*2 is equal to the logarithm of the ratio of scheduled commercial bank deposits to the output in a region. *OPEN*1 is the ratio of exports plus imports to GDP. *OPEN*2 is the ratio of net foreign direct investment to GDP. *INF* is equal to the growth rate of the WPI. *y* is the growth rate of the per capita output in each state.

rate. With respect to the influence of the measure of openness on the poverty ratio, the table reveals that the coefficients of the trade to GDP ratio (*OPEN*1) are estimated to be positive (0.002 for Model 1 and 0.003 for Model 3) and are statistically significant at the 1% level. The empirical results also indicate that the coefficients of the net inflow of foreign direct investment to GDP ratio (*OPEN*2) are estimated to be positive (0.039 for Model 2 and 0.055 for Model 4) and are statistically significant at the 5% level. Our results show that the poverty ratio increases as the degree of openness increases.

Next, we examine the effects of inflation on the poverty ratio. The coefficients of inflation (*INF*) are estimated to be positive (0.327 for Model 1,

0.394 for Model 2, 0.440 for Model 3, and 0.535 for Model 4) and are statistically significant at the 1% level for all cases. Thus, a higher inflation rate increases, and therefore, worsens the poverty ratio.

Furthermore, we analyze the effects of the regional variable on the poverty ratio. This study uses regional growth rate as the regional variable. As the table shows, the coefficients of the regional growth rate of output (y) are estimated to be negative (-0.997 for Model 1, -0.968 for Model 2, -1.581 for Model 3, and -1.543 for Model 4) and are statistically significant at the 1% level. Our results indicate that an increase in regional growth rate decreases, and therefore, improves the poverty ratio.

Finally, Table 7.3 reports the J-statistic and its associated p-value for each model. The J-statistic is used as a test of over-identifying moment conditions. As is clear from the table, the over-identifying restriction cannot be rejected at the 5% significance level, and thus the model specification is empirically supported.

7.5.2   Results for the urban areas

Table 7.4 reports the empirical results when we use the poverty ratio for the urban areas. As is clear from this table, the coefficients of the credit to regional output ratio ($FD1$) are estimated to be negative (-6.194 for Model 1 and -6.693 for Model 2) and are statistically significant at the 1% level. The empirical results indicate that the coefficients of the deposits to regional output ratio ($FD2$) are estimated to be negative (-6.081 for Model 3 and -6.441 for Model 4) and are statistically significant at the 1% level. Our results reveal that the poverty ratio for the urban areas decreases as the financial system deepens.

Next, we examine the influence of the openness measure on the poverty ratio. The table reveals that the coefficients of the trade to GDP ratio ($OPEN1$) are estimated to be positive (0.004 for Model 1 and 0.005 for Model 3) and are statistically significant at the 1% level. The empirical results also indicate that the coefficients of the net inflow of foreign direct investment to GDP ratio ($OPEN2$) are estimated to be positive (0.096 for Model 2 and 0.114 for Model 4) and are statistically significant at the 1% level. Our results show that the poverty ratio for the urban areas increases as the degree of openness increases.

Table 7.4   Financial Deepening and Poverty: Urban Areas

	Model 1	Model 2	Model 3	Model 4
POV (−1)	0.100	0.103	0.205	0.240
	(0.024)**	(0.037)**	(0.001)***	(0.001)***
*FD*1	−6.194	−6.693		
	(0.000)***	(0.000)***		
*FD*2			−6.081	−6.441
			(0.000)***	(0.000)***
*OPEN*1	0.004		0.005	
	(0.000)***		(0.000)***	
*OPEN*2		0.096		0.114
		(0.000)***		(0.000)***
INF	0.109	0.235	0.135	0.284
	(0.028)**	(0.000)***	(0.027)**	(0.000)***
y	−1.413	−1.349	−1.775	−1.764
	(0.000)***	(0.000)***	(0.000)***	(0.000)***
J-statistic	16.151	13.978	18.158	16.140
	(0.241)	(0.375)	(0.152)	(0.242)
Number of Observations	124	124	124	124

Notes: (1) Numbers in parentheses are *p*-values.
(2) Significance at the 1% and 5% level is indicated by *** and **, respectively.
(3) The dependent variable is the poverty ratio (*POV*). *FD*1 is equal to the logarithm of the ratio of scheduled commercial bank credit to the output in a region. *FD*2 is equal to the logarithm of the ratio of scheduled commercial bank deposits to the output in a region. *OPEN*1 is the ratio of exports plus imports to GDP. *OPEN*2 is the ratio of net foreign direct investment to GDP. *INF* is equal to the growth rate of the WPI. *y* is the growth rate of the per capita output in each state.

Third, we analyze the effects of inflation on the poverty ratio. The coefficients of inflation (*INF*) are estimated to be positive (0.109 for Model 1, 0.235 for Model 2, 0.135 for Model 3, and 0.284 for Model 4) and are statistically significant at the 5% level for Models 1 and 3 and at the 1% level for Models 2 and 4. Thus, an increase in the inflation rate worsens the poverty ratio in the urban areas.

Furthermore, we analyze the effects of the regional growth rate on the poverty ratio. As the table shows, the coefficients of the regional growth rate of output (*y*) are estimated to be negative (−1.413 for Model 1, −1.349 for Model 2, −1.775 for Model 3, and −1.764 for Model 4) and are statistically significant at the 1% level. Our results indicate that an increase in the regional growth rate improves the poverty ratio in the urban areas.

Finally, as is clear from the table, the over-identifying restriction cannot be rejected at the 5% significance level, and thus the model specification is empirically supported. The results in Table 7.4 are consistent with those shown in Table 7.3.

7.5.3   Results for the rural areas

Table 7.5 reports the empirical results when we use the poverty ratio for the rural areas. First, we analyze the effects of financial deepening (*FD*1 or *FD*2) on the poverty ratio. As is clear from this table, the coefficients of financial deepening are estimated to be negative (-8.674 for Model 1, -8.517 for Model 2, -9.890 for Model 3, and -9.979 for Model 4) and are

Table 7.5   Financial Deepening and Poverty: Rural Areas

	Model 1	Model 2	Model 3	Model 4
POV(−1)	−0.044	−0.099	−0.176	−0.249
	(0.470)	(0.086)*	(0.067)*	(0.001)***
*FD*1	−8.674	−8.517		
	(0.000)***	(0.000)***		
*FD*2			−9.890	−9.979
			(0.000)***	(0.000)***
*OPEN*1	0.003		0.003	
	(0.000)***		(0.002)***	
*OPEN*2		0.047		0.060
		(0.012)**		(0.013)**
INF	0.299	0.395	0.397	0.510
	(0.000)***	(0.000)***	(0.000)***	(0.000)***
y	−1.180	−1.118	−1.647	−1.601
	(0.000)***	(0.000)***	(0.000)***	(0.000)***
J-statistic	20.523	19.720	18.965	18.078
	(0.083)	(0.102)	(0.124)	(0.155)
Number of Observations	124	124	124	124

Notes: (1) Numbers in parentheses are *p*-values.
(2) Significance at the 1%, 5%, and 10% level is indicated by ***, **, and *, respectively.
(3) The dependent variable is the poverty ratio (*POV*). *FD*1 is equal to the logarithm of the ratio of scheduled commercial bank credit to the output in a region. *FD*2 is equal to the logarithm of the ratio of scheduled commercial bank deposits to the output in a region. *OPEN*1 is the ratio of exports plus imports to GDP. *OPEN*2 is the ratio of net foreign direct investment to GDP. *INF* is equal to the growth rate of the WPI. *y* is the growth rate of the per capita output in each state.

statistically significant at the 1% level for all cases. Our results reveal that the poverty ratio for the rural areas decreases as the financial system deepens.

Next, we examine the influence of the measure of openness (*OPEN*1 or *OPEN*2) on the poverty ratio. The empirical results indicate that the coefficients of the measure of openness are estimated to be positive (0.003 for Model 1, 0.047 for Model 2, 0.003 for Model 3, and 0.060 for Model 4) and are statistically significant at the 1% level for Models 1 and 3 and at the 5% level for Models 2 and 4. Our results show that the poverty ratio for the rural areas increases as the degree of openness increases.

Third, we analyze the effects of inflation on the poverty ratio. The coefficients of inflation (*INF*) are estimated to be positive (0.299 for Model 1, 0.395 for Model 2, 0.397 for Model 3, and 0.510 for Model 4) and are statistically significant at the 1% level for all cases. Thus, an increase in the inflation rate worsens the poverty ratio in the rural areas.

Furthermore, we analyze the effects of the regional growth rate on the poverty ratio. As the table shows, the coefficients of the regional growth rate of output (y) are estimated to be negative (-1.180 for Model 1, -1.118 for Model 2, -1.647 for Model 3, and -1.601 for Model 4) and are statistically significant at the 1% level for all cases. Our results indicate that an increase in the regional growth rate improves the poverty ratio in the rural areas.

Finally, as is clear from the table, the over-identifying restriction cannot be rejected at the 5% significance level, and thus the model specification is empirically supported. The results given in Table 7.5 are consistent with those shown in Tables 7.3 and 7.4.

7.5.4 Summary

Table 7.6 summarizes the empirical results of this study. Financial deepening and economic growth improve the poverty ratio, whereas international

Table 7.6   Summary of Empirical Results

Explanatory and Control Variable	Effect on Poverty Ratio
Financial Deepening	Decreases (improves)
International Openness	Increases (worsens)
Inflation	Increases (worsens)
Economic Growth	Decreases (improves)

openness and inflation worsen the poverty ratio. Our results for financial deepening, inflation, and economic growth are typically consistent with those of prior research.

7.6 Concluding Remarks

A number of studies hitherto conducted to examine the finance-growth nexus have suggested that the development of financial intermediaries con- tributes to economic growth (e.g., King and Levine, 1993a, 1993b; Rajan and Zingales, 1998; Levine *et al.*, 2000). Moreover, given the close rela- tionship between finance and growth, a growing body of empirical work has analyzed the effect of financial deepening on poverty reduction for a variety of countries and regions. The principal objective of this chapter is to investigate this issue empirically for the country with the largest poor population, India. In our empirical analysis, we consider models in which the poverty ratio is explained by financial deepening, controlling for inter- national openness, inflation rate, and economic growth. We then estimate the models by using unbalanced panel data on 28 Indian states and union territories for seven time periods (1973, 1977, 1983, 1987, 1993, 1999, and 2004). From a dynamic GMM estimation, we obtain the following main findings.

First, financial deepening statistically leads to the reduction of poverty ratio in the whole economy and, separately, in urban and rural areas. Considering that we measured financial deepening by the credit amount or deposit amount of the scheduled commercial banks, this result indi- cates that the development of the banking sector has been beneficial for the poor in India. Our results are generally in line with those of existing studies, including Honohan (2004), Jalilian and Kirkpatrick (2005), Beck *et al.* (2007), and Jeanneney and Kpodar (2008), albeit based on different samples and econometric techniques.

Second, like financial deepening, the coefficient of economic growth is estimated to have a significant negative value in the whole economy as well as in urban and rural areas. This implies that economic growth increases not only the country's average income but also the income of the poor. Since the early 1990s, the country has witnessed a clear trend of rising inequality, after a flat phase in urban areas and a declining tendency in rural areas previously (Datt and Ravallion, 2009, p. 18). Our results indicate that, in spite of the recent increase in inequality, economic growth actually helps alleviate poverty. Using decomposition analysis, Bhanumurthy and Mitra (2004) observed that the growth/mean effect, rather than the inequality effect and the population shift effect, accounts for much of the decline in poverty in most of their sample states over the years from FY 1983 to FY 1993 and from FY 1993 to FY 1999. Besides, Datt and Ravallion (2009) also found, regressing the poverty measure on either per capita consumption or income, that economic growth tended to reduce poverty in India over the period from 1958 to 2006. Accordingly, our result seems to be consistent with these previous findings.

Third, a rise in international openness significantly leads to the increase in poverty ratio in the whole economy and in urban and rural areas taken separately. This result holds in cases where international openness was measured by either *OPEN*1 or *OPEN*2. The impact of economic globalization on poverty is still an important topic debated in the literature. For example, Dollar and Kraay (2004) showed that changes in trade volume have a strong positive relationship with changes in the growth rate for roughly 100 countries. Taking into account the evidence from Dollar and Kraay (2002), they stated that the increase in growth rates accompanying expanded trade generally translates into proportional increases in the income of the poor. Meanwhile, Milanovic (2005) estimated pooled cross-country regressions relating trade and financial openness to relative incomes across 138 decile shares in three time periods and found that it is the rich who benefit from trade openness at very low national income levels but as income levels rise the incomes of the poor and the middle class rise proportionately more than the incomes of the rich (Milanovic, 2005, p. 40). Partly consistent with the latter study, our result indicates that international openness may hurt the poor in both rural and urban areas, implying that the current trend of economic globalization supported by Anglo-Saxon capitalism is not the method for solving poverty at the present time in India.[9]

Finally, the coefficient of the inflation rate is estimated to have a significant positive value in the whole economy and in both urban and rural

---

[9]Further research may be necessary to analyze whether a nonlinear relationship exists between economic globalization and poverty in India, as stressed by Agenor (2002).

areas; this suggests that inflation has an adverse effect on poverty in India. This result is in line with most comparable findings in the literature. For example, Romer and Romer (1998) examined the relationship between the long-run performance of monetary policy and the average income of the poor by using cross-country regression and found that low inflation as well as stable growth in aggregate demand is associated with improved well-being of the poor for a large sample of countries.[10] In the Indian debate, Datt and Ravallion (1998) attempted to explain the deviations from the trend rates of progress in reducing rural poverty by using pooled state-level data for the period from 1957 to 1991, and pointed out that the rural poor are adversely affected in the short run by rising inflation. Datt and Ravallion (2002) and Pradhan (2008) also drew a similar conclusion to Datt and Ravallion (1998).[11]

In sum, we conclude from the above results that further financial deepening as well as rapid economic growth will become an important priority for India as it attempts to reduce poverty. Since the start of economic reforms in the early 1990s, India has promoted financial deepening to a large extent. In fact, the credit and deposit amounts of the scheduled commercial banks, given as shares of real GDP, have increased, respectively, from 6.6% and 10.4% in the 1980s to 16.9% and 30.8% in the 1990s, and to 83.1% and 114.8% in 2008. However, when these banks are categorized by region, such as metropolitan, urban, semi-urban, and rural, metropolitan areas, show the highest rates of growth, while the gaps between metropolitan and other areas have expanded over time, especially since the 1990s.

---

[10]Besides, Easterly and Fischer (2001) found, using pooled cross-country samples, that direct measures of the well-being of the poor, such as the change in their share of the national income, the percentage decline in the poverty ratio, and the percentage change in the real minimum wage, are negatively correlated with the inflation rate.

[11]Datt and Ravallion (2002) empirically analyzed how the poverty ratio is affected by the relevant variables, using unbalanced panel data for 15 Indian states from 1960 to 1994. They found that a higher inflation rate increases the incidence of poverty, while higher farm yield, state government spending, and non-agricultural output per person reduces the poverty ratio. Moreover, Pradhan (2008), in an investigation of the determinants of rural poverty in India from FY 1987 to FY 1999, observed that the consumer price index for agricultural laborers has a positive causal effect, suggesting that an increase in food prices leads to an increase in rural poverty.

Recently, the Indian government has attempted to achieve faster and more inclusive growth so that all people, including the poor and the weaker sections of society, equitably receive the benefits of growth. Following this, in April 2005, the RBI formally announced that financial inclusion would be one of its policy objectives. It has since undertaken various initiatives to ensure access to and usage of formal financial services for all people, especially hitherto excluded people, at an affordable cost.[12] These measures are expected to promote financial deepening by expanding the reach of banking facilities to wider sections of the population and, given our empirical results, to contribute to poverty reduction.

In addition, the empirical results in this study indicate that, to make progress on poverty reduction, Indian authorities should also consider the negative impact of higher inflation and more international openness on the poor. Although the RBI defines the pursuit of price stability and economic growth as its ultimate objectives, controlling inflation is not an easy task for India. This is partly because the inflation rate is subject to both demand and supply shocks under rapid economic growth (Singh, 2006, p. 2961). Regardless of the difficulties, however, the central bank urgently needs to tackle inflationary pressure from the perspective of poverty alleviation. Moreover, with regard to international openness, it is inevitable that India will further integrate into the global economy through trade and capital liberalization and economic growth. Therefore, the government will be increasingly required to support the people who are adversely affected by globalization.

References

Agenor, P.R., 2002. Does globalization hurt the poor? World Bank Policy Research Working Paper 2922, The World Bank, Washington, DC.

Ang, J.B., 2010. Finance and inequality: The case of India. *Southern Economic Journal* 76, 738–761.

---

[12]For example, the RBI advised the commercial banks to make available a basic "no-frills" banking account with a low or nil minimum balance requirement and charges, introduce a General Credit Card facility in rural and semi-urban areas, and simplify the know-your-customer procedure for those accounts with small balances and lower credit limits (Leeladhar, 2008, pp. 1508–1509; RBI, 2008, pp. 306, 308).

Apergis, N., Filippidis, I., Economidou, C., 2007. Financial deepening and economic growth linkages: A panel data analysis. *Review of World Economics* 143, 179–198.

Arellano, M., Bond, S., 1991. Some tests of specification for panel data: Monte Carlo evidence and an application to employment equations. *Review of Economic Studies* 58, 277–297.

Beck, T., Demirgüç-Kunt, A., Levine, R., 2004. Finance, inequality, and poverty: Cross-country evidence. NBER Working Paper 10979, The National Bureau of Economic Research, Cambridge, MA.

Beck, T., Demirgüç-Kunt, A., Levine, R., 2007. Finance, inequality and the poor. *Journal of Economic Growth* 12, 27–49.

Bhanumurthy, N.R., Mitra, A., 2004. Economic growth, poverty, and inequality in Indian states in the pre-reform and reform periods. *Asian Development Review* 21, 79–99.

Bhattacharya, P.C., Sivasubramanian, M.N., 2003. Financial development and economic growth in India. *Applied Financial Economics* 13, 905–909.

Chen, S., Ravallion, M., 2008. The developing world is poorer than we thought, but no less successful in the tight against poverty. World Bank Policy Research Working Paper 4703, The World Bank, Washington, DC.

Clarke, G.R.G., Xu, L.C., Zou, H-F., 2006. Finance and income inequality: What do the data tell us? *Southern Economic Journal* 72, 578–596.

Datt, G., Ravallion, M., 1998. Why have some Indian states done better than others at reducing rural poverty? *Economica* 65, 17–38.

Datt, G., Ravallion, M., 2002. Is India's economic growth leaving the poor behind? *Journal of Economic Perspectives* 16, 89–108.

Datt, G., Ravallion, M., 2009. Has India's economic growth become more pro-poor in the wake of economic reforms? World Bank Policy Research Working Paper 5103, The World Bank, Washington, DC.

Davis, D.R., Mishra, P., 2007. Stolper–Samuelson is dead and other crimes of both theory and data, in: Harrison, A. (Eds.), *Globalization and Poverty*. The University of Chicago Press, Chicago, pp. 87–107.

Demetriades, P.O., Hussein, K.A., 1996. Does financial development cause economic growth? Time-series evidence from 16 countries. *Journal of Development Economics* 51, 387–411.

Demirgüç-Kunt, A., Maksimovic, V., 1996. Financial constraints, uses of funds, and firm growth: An international comparison. World Bank Policy Research Working Paper 1671, The World Bank, Washington, DC.

Dollar, D., Kraay, A., 2002. Growth is good for the poor. *Journal of Economic Growth* 7, 195–225.

Dollar, D., Kraay, A., 2004. Trade, growth, and poverty. *Economic Journal* 114, F22–F49.

Easterly, W., Fischer, S., 2001. Inflation and the poor. *Journal of Money, Credit and Banking* 33, 160–178.

Harrison, A., McMillan, M., 2007. On the links between globalization and poverty. *Journal of Economic Inequality* 5, 123–134.

Himanshu, 2007. Recent trends in poverty and inequality: Some preliminary results. *Economic and Political Weekly* 42, 497–508.

Holden, P., Prokopenko, V., 2001. Financial development and poverty alleviation: Issues and policy implications for developing and transition countries. IMF Working Paper WP/01/160, International Monetary Fund, Washington, DC.

Honohan, P., 2004. Financial development, growth and poverty: How close are the links? World Bank Policy Research Working Paper 3203, The World Bank, Washington, DC.

Jalilian, H., Kirkpatrick, C., 2002. Financial development and poverty reduction in developing countries. *International Journal of Finance & Economics* 7, 97–108.

Jalilian, H., Kirkpatrick, C., 2005. Does financial development contribute to poverty reduction? *Journal of Development Studies* 41, 636–656.

Jeanneney, S.G., Kpodar, K., 2008. Financial development and poverty reduction: Can there be a benefit without a cost? IMF Working Paper WP/08/62, International Monetary Fund, Washington, DC.

Kai, H., Hamori, S., 2009. Globalization, financial depth, and inequality in Sub-Saharan Africa. *Economics Bulletin* 29, 2025–2037.

King, R., Levine, R., 1993a. Finance and growth: Schumpeter might be right. *The Quarterly Journal of Economics* 108, 717–737.

King, R., Levine, R., 1993b. Finance, entrepreneurship and growth: Theory and evidence. *Journal of Monetary Economics* 32, 513–542.

Kirkpatrick, C., 2000. Financial development, economic growth, and poverty reduction. *The Pakistan Development Review* 39, 363–388.

Leeladhar, V., 2008. The Indian banking industry — A retrospect of selected aspects. *RBI Monthly Bulletin September*, Reserve Bank of India, Mumbai, 1501–1510.

Levine, R., Zervos, S., 1998. Stock markets, banks and economic growth. *American Economic Review* 88, 537–558.

Levine, R., Loayza, N.V., Beck, T., 2000. Financial intermediation and growth: Causality and causes. *Journal of Monetary Economics* 46, 31–77.

Li, H., Squire, L., Zou, H-F., 1998. Explaining international and intertemporal variations in income inequality. *Economic Journal* 108, 26–43.

Luintel, K.B., Khan, M., 1999. A quantitative reassessment of the finance-growth nexus: Evidence from a multivariate VAR. *Journal of Development Economics* 60, 381–405.

Milanovic, B., 2005. Can we discern the effect of globalization on income distribution? Evidence from household surveys. *World Bank Economic Review* 19, 21–44.

Odhiambo, N.M., 2009. Finance-growth-poverty nexus in South Africa: A dynamic causality linkage. *The Journal of Socio-Economics* 38, 320–325.

Odhiambo, N.M., 2010. Financial deepening and poverty reduction in Zambia: An empirical investigation. *International Journal of Social Economics* 37, 41–53.

Pradhan, R.P., 2008. Rural poverty in India: The trends and determinants. *The Indian Journal of Economics* 88, 377–391.

Quartey, P., 2008. Financial sector development, savings mobilization and poverty reduction in Ghana, in: Guha-Khasnobis, B., Mavrotas, G. (Eds.), *Financial Development, Institutions, Growth and Poverty Reduction*. Palgrave Macmillan, Basingstoke, pp. 87–119.

Rajan, R.G., Zingales, L., 1998. Financial dependence and growth. *American Economic Review* 88, 559–586.

Reserve Bank of India (RBI), 1995. *Annual Report 1994–95*. RBI, Mumbai.

Reserve Bank of India (RBI), 2008. Financial inclusion, in: *Report on Currency and Finance 2007–08*. RBI, Mumbai, pp. 294–348.

Reserve Bank of India (RBI), 2009. *Handbook on Statistics of Indian Economy 2008–09*. RBI, Mumbai.

Reserve Bank of India (RBI), various issues. *Banking Statistics: Basic Statistical Returns*. RBI, Mumbai.

Reserve Bank of India (RBI), various issues. *Basic Statistical Returns of Scheduled Commercial Banks in India*. RBI, Mumbai.

Romer, C.D., Romer, D.H., 1998. Monetary policy and the well-being of the poor. NBER Working Paper 6793, The National Bureau of Economic Research, Cambridge MA.

Sen, K., Vaidya, R.R., 1997. *The Process of Financial Liberalization in India*. Oxford University Press, Delhi.

Singh, K., 2006. Inflation targeting: International experience and prospects for India. *Economic and Political Weekly* 41, 2958–2961.

Topalova, P., 2005. Trade liberalization, poverty and inequality: Evidence from Indian districts. NBER Working Paper 11614, The National Bureau of Economic Research, Cambridge, MA.

Wade, R.H., 2004. Is globalization reducing poverty and inequality? *World Development* 32, 567–589.

World Bank, 2001. *World Development Report 2000/2001*. Oxford University Press, New York.

World Bank, 2008. *World Development Indicators 2008*. The World Bank, Washington, DC.

Chapter 8

Financial Inclusion and Poverty Alleviation in India

8.1 Introduction

There is much evidence for a strong and causal relationship between the depth of the financial system on the one hand, and investment, growth, and total factor productivity on the other (Claessens, 2005, p. 2). Much of this evidence has focused on the importance of overall financial development, which is typically referred to as "financial deepening" and is perceived as the increased scale of the financial sector in the real economy. In many developing countries, however, the financial system does not largely cater to the needs of all customers and tends to be skewed towards those already better off (*ibid.*, p. 2). Accordingly, in addition to financial deepening, "financial inclusion" has received a great deal of attention as of late.

Generally speaking, financial inclusion can be defined as the process of ensuring access to and usage of basic formal financial services for all people at an affordable cost. Basic formal financial services include credit, savings, insurance, payments, and remittance facilities. Without access to these services, people often resort to using high-cost informal financial sources, and financial exclusion likely exerts a disproportionally negative impact on low-income groups. Therefore, the promotion of financial inclusion is considered to play an important role in alleviating poverty and reducing income inequalities within a country.

In India, the concept of financial inclusion can be traced back to the social control of the banking sector that started in the 1960s. Since then, various measures have been undertaken to promote financial inclusion. In April 2005, the Reserve Bank of India (RBI) formally announced that financial inclusion would be one of its primary policy objectives. This announcement brought more attention to the issue and sparked growth in the literature on financial inclusion in India. Several empirical studies have focused on the degree of progress in financial inclusion and have examined its relation to relevant variables such as economic growth and infrastructure development. Based on these previous studies, this chapter aims to empirically analyze the link between financial inclusion and poverty reduction by using panel data from 25 Indian states and union territories from FY 1973 to FY 2004.

The chapter is organized as follows: Section 8.2 summarizes the history of financial inclusion measures in India. Section 8.3 examines developments in financial inclusion and the poverty ratio, and Section 8.4 reviews relevant prior research. We then present an empirical analysis of the possible relationship between financial inclusion and poverty reduction. Section 8.5 provides a brief explanation of the model and the definitions and sources of the data, and Section 8.6 shows the empirical results. Lastly, the concluding remarks summarize the main findings of the study.

8.2   A History of Financial Inclusion in India

Since the late 1960s, India has undertaken various initiatives to expand formal financial services to rural areas (RBI, 2008, p. 303). These could be broadly categorized into the following three time phases by their characteristics: the first phase running throughout the 1980s, the second phase spanning the early 1990s through March 2005, and the third phase beginning in April 2005 (*ibid.*, p. 304).

During the first phase of financial inclusion initiated by bank nationalization in 1969, some measures were taken at different points in time to expand the outreach of banking facilities and increase the flow of credit to rural areas (*ibid.*, p. 303). These measures were mainly composed of the implementation of the branch licensing policy, the establishment of Regional Rural Banks (RRBs), and the introduction of priority sector lending. For example, the branch licensing policy put emphasis on the expansion of banking facilities in rural and unbanked areas, and in fact, it contributed toward promoting branch openings in rural and semi-urban areas, thus increasing the share of total branches from 62.6% in 1969 to 77.2% in 1990 (Rao, 2007, pp. 355–356). Also, the RRBs that the commercial banks set up in 1975 to cater to the credit needs of the rural poor successfully expanded their branch network in rural areas and comprised more than 40.0% of the total number of rural branches of commercial banks, although this advance was limited in that it constituted only around 2.0% of banking sector credits (Joshi, 2006, pp. 85, 92). Moreover, under priority sector lending, bank credit extended to priority sectors, such as agriculture, small-scale industries, industrial estates, road and water operators, retail traders, small businesses, professionals, self-employed persons, education, and weaker sections, increased from Rs. 659 crore (18.2% of the total net bank credit) in 1969 to Rs. 40,475 crore (42.4%) in 1989 (Shajahan, 1998, pp. 2750–2751). The number of priority sector accounts also increased from 7.8 lakhs to 331 lakhs during the same period (*ibid.*, p. 2751).

With the onset of the economic reforms of the early 1990s, however, systematic financial sector reforms were implemented which placed more emphasis on the efficiency and profitability of the banking system, which had allegedly been neglected in earlier decades (Chavan, 2007, p. 3219). As a result, attempts towards financial inclusion also underwent significant modification in the 1990s. Specifically, in 1991, the branch licensing policy was relaxed, and banks were allowed to close down loss-making branches in urban, metropolitan, and rural centers in cases where these centers were being served by two other commercial banks excluding the RRBs (Sen and Vaidya, 1997, p. 43).[1] Also, in 1992, the RRBs were permitted to lend 40.0% of fresh advances to their clients outside the target groups, such as small and marginal farmers, agricultural laborers, and artisans, and this proportion was increased to 60.0% of fresh lending from 1994 (Joshi, 2006, p. 88). Moreover, coverage of priority sectors was increased by adding many new sectors and segments, thus indirectly affecting the share of credit to areas traditionally deemed priority sectors when the concept was first introduced (Rao, 2007, p. 356).

While these state-controlled initiatives were de-emphasized, in the second phase, financial inclusion was encouraged mainly by the promotion of microfinance through the Self- Help Group (SHG)-Bank Linkage Program

---

[1] In October 2009, the RBI took a momentous step by freeing bank branch openings in towns and villages with populations of up to 50,000, while the scheduled commercial banks (other than the RRBs) were enjoined to ensure that at least one-third of such branch expansions take place in underbanked districts of underbanked states (Subbarao, 2010, p. 5).

(SBLP) (RBI, 2008, p. 304). This program was launched by the National Bank for Agriculture and Rural Development in 1992 to facilitate collective decision making by the poor and to provide "door step" banking (*ibid.*, p. 305). Under the program, financially excluded people, especially poor women, can establish SHGs, engage in promoting their banking habits, and conduct transactions with banks, i.e., credit and deposit facilities. Since its inception, the SBLP has seen rapid expansion. As of March 2007, 50 commercial banks, 96 RRBs, and 352 cooperative banks participated in this program, and the number of bank-linked SHGs increased from 255 in FY 1992 to 29 lakhs in FY 2006, while cumulative bank loans increased from Rs. 0.3 crore to Rs. 18,047 crore during the same period (*ibid.*, p. 330). During the second phase, Kisan Credit Cards (KCCs) were also introduced to provide adequate and timely credit from the banking sector to farmers, who would then be able to purchase agricultural inputs and draw cash for their production needs (RBI, 1999, 1.25). In every year since its introduction, 80 to 90 lakh KCCs have been issued, and in FY 2007, the cumulative number of KCCs amounted to 761 lakhs.

The third phase of financial inclusion began in April 2005, when the RBI explicitly used the term financial inclusion as a major policy objective in their Annual Policy Statement for FY 2005 (RBI, 2008, p. 304). In this statement, while recognizing concerns that banking practices tended to exclude vast sections of the population, in particular, the pensioners, the self-employed, and those employed in the unorganized sector, the RBI urged banks to review their existing practices and provide banking services to all segments of the population on an equitable basis (RBI, 2005, p. 40; Leeladhar, 2006, p. 76).

For example, the RBI advised banks to introduce a basic "no-frills" banking account with low or nil minimum balance and charges so as to expand the outreach of such accounts to vast sections of the population.[2] The RBI also directed banks to consider the introduction of a General Credit Card facility in rural and semi-urban areas. With a view to providing

---

[2]In August 2012, the RBI directed banks to rechristen no-frills banking accounts as Basic Savings Bank Deposit Accounts (BSBDAs), with a view to further encourage the opening of such accounts and to integrate them into basic banking services (RBI, 2012, p. 14). As a result, all existing no-frills accounts were converted to BSBDAs.

hassle-free credit, this facility entitles the holder to withdraw money up to the credit limit of Rs. 25,000 without insistence on security or purpose (Leeladhar, 2008, p. 1509). Moreover, in order to ensure that persons belonging to low-income groups do not encounter difficulties in opening bank accounts, the know-your-customer procedure for opening accounts was simplified for those accounts with balances not exceeding Rs. 50,000 and credit limits not exceeding Rs. 100,000 annually (RBI, 2008, p. 306).

Have these initiatives actually encouraged access to and/or usage of formal financial services in India? The All India Debt and Investment Survey (AIDIS) by the National Sample Survey Organization (NSSO) indicates some interesting features on progress in financial inclusion by analyzing patterns of household debt (see Tables 8.1 and 8.2). Table 8.1 shows the number of households indebted to different credit agencies. The number of households indebted to institutional sources increased sharply between 1961 and 1991 in rural areas and between 1981 and 1991 in urban areas in absolute terms as well as in terms of the share of total indebted households. A detailed analysis suggests that this finding can be explained mainly by the high growth in households indebted to commercial banks. Thereafter, the number of households indebted to institutional agencies continued to

Table 8.1   Number of Indebted Households (Number in Lakhs)

	Rural			Urban		
	Institutional Agencies	Non-institutional Agencies	Total	Institutional Agencies	Non-institutional Agencies	Total
1961	75 (17.4)	356 (82.6)	431	NA	NA	NA
1971	76 (23.9)	242 (76.0)	318	NA	NA	NA
1981	89 (49.0)	93 (51.2)	182	23 (45.6)	27 (53.5)	50
1991	181 (66.7)	114 (41.9)	271	50 (61.1)	39 (48.7)	81
2002	198 (50.6)	229 (58.5)	392	52 (52.2)	52 (52.8)	99

Sources: NSSO (1998a, 1998b, 2005) and RBI (1965, 1977, 1987, 2008).

Notes: (1) Institutional agencies are composed of the government, cooperative societies, and commercial banks, whereas non-institutional agencies are composed of landlords, agricultural moneylenders, and professional moneylenders.

(2) Figures in parentheses show the percentage for total number of indebted households.

(3) NA indicates that there are no relevant data.

Table 8.2   Outstanding Household Debt (Amount in Rs. Crores)

	Rural			Urban		
	Institutional Agencies	Non-institutional Agencies	Total	Institutional Agencies	Non-institutional Agencies	Total
1961	413 (14.8)	2,376 (85.2)	2,789	NA	NA	NA
1971	1,094 (29.2)	2,658 (70.8)	3,752	NA	NA	NA
1981	3,794 (61.3)	2,399 (38.7)	6,193	1,813 (60.0)	1,210 (40.0)	3,023
1991	14,215 (64.0)	7,996 (36.0)	22,211	10,662 (70.0)	4,570 (30.0)	15,232
2002	63,648 (57.1)	47,820 (42.9)	111,468	49,060 (75.1)	16,266 (24.9)	65,327

Source: RBI (2008).

Notes: (1) Institutional agencies are composed of the government, cooperative societies, and commercial banks, whereas non-institutional agencies are composed of landlords, agricultural moneylenders, and professional moneylenders.
(2) Figures in parentheses show the percentage for total outstanding of household debt.
(3) NA indicates that there are no relevant data.

increase, although the share of institutional sources declined between 1991 and 2002 in both rural and urban areas, with a concurrent increase in the share of non-institutional sources.

We can also find similar trends in the pattern of households' outstanding debts in Table 8.2. Specifically, the proportion of household debt owed to institutional sources increased in both rural and urban areas in absolute terms. This was mainly due to the high growth in households' debts to commercial banks. In relative terms, however, the share of debt owed to institutional sources by rural households declined between 1991 and 2002, while that of non-institutional sources increased correspondingly. These trends in institutional and non-institutional credit sources can be taken to imply that financial inclusion in India has been successfully promoted to a certain extent, although the results are still far from satisfactory.

8.3   Financial Inclusion and Poverty Conditions

In the Section 8.2, we showed that a variety of initiatives have been taken to expand financial services in rural India, mainly through commercial banks. In addition, according to data from the AIDIS, we found that institutional sources increased with regard to household debt, with commercial banks playing a leading role. Hence, this section first examines the movements for financial inclusion in India from the early 1980s by using relevant data on commercial banks. This section also reviews how poverty conditions changed during the surveyed period, because poverty reduction is one of the major goals of financial inclusion.

Since access to financial services is not synonymous with their use, it is necessary to distinguish between these two different concepts, namely, the access to or the possibility of using financial services and the actual use of financial services (Beck *et al.*, 2007b, p. 236). Following Beck *et al.* (2007b), we regard the number of bank branches as the indicator for measuring physical access to formal financial services, while the number of bank accounts is utilized as a measure of the actual use of formal financial services.

In India, the scheduled commercial banks steadily increased the number of their branches from 8,262 in 1969 to 77,699 in 2008. Figure 8.1 illustrates the population group-wise distribution of commercial bank branches during the period 1969 to 2008.[3] In all areas, rural branches showed the most

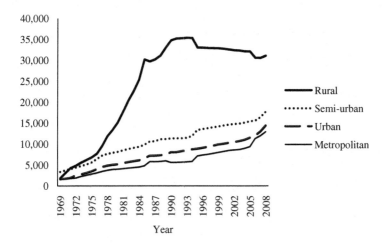

Figure 8.1   Population Group-wise Distribution of Commercial Bank Branches (Number)
Source: RBI (2009).

---

[3]Population groups such as, rural, semi-urban, urban, and metropolitan, are defined as places having populations of under 9,999; 10,000 to 99,999; 100,000 to 999,999; and over 1,000,000 respectively (RBI, 2009, p. 483).

growth and reached their peak of 35,389 (57.9%) in 1993. Subsequently, however, they started to decrease and so did their share of total branches. These results are considered to reflect the changes in the branch licensing policy since the early 1990s, which were discussed earlier. In contrast, bank branches in other areas, such as semi-urban, urban, and metropolitan, increased even after the 1990s and steadily expanded their shares in total. As of March 2008, the number of bank branches in metropolitan areas is the smallest among all areas, but the average growth rate in these areas was the highest from 1990 to 2008.

Next, we move on to examine another measure of financial inclusion: the actual use of financial services. The total number of credit accounts increased from 43 lakhs in 1972 to 11 crore in 2008, whereas the total number of deposit accounts increased from 3.5 crore to 58 crore during the same period. Figures 8.2 and 8.3 illustrate the population group-wise distribution of credit accounts and deposit accounts respectively, during the period 1980 to 2008. In the last three decades, the number of credit accounts was volatile in all areas, especially in rural and metropolitan areas (see Figure 8.2). That is, during the 1980s, the number of credit accounts increased in all areas, especially in rural areas. Entering the 1990s, however, they showed decreasing or stagnant trends across all areas and recorded the highest rates of reduction in rural areas. Since 2000, credit accounts again

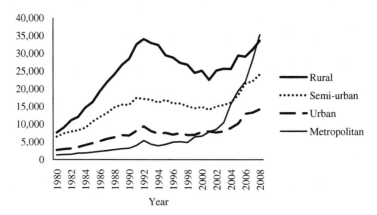

Figure 8.2   Population Group-wise Distribution of Credit Accounts (Accounts in Thousands)

Source: RBI (2009).

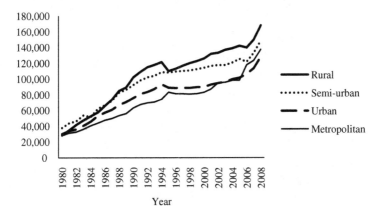

Figure 8.3 Population Group-wise Distribution of Deposit Accounts (Accounts in Thousands)

Source: RBI (2009).

began to increase in all areas and registered the highest rates of growth in metropolitan areas. In March 2008, the number of credit accounts in metropolitan areas exceeded that in rural areas for the first time. Compared to credit accounts, deposit accounts have shown relatively steady growth trends (see Figure 8.3). Even in the 1990s, the growth rates remained positive in all areas though they were lower relative to those in the 1980s. Of all areas, the metropolitan areas showed the highest growth rates in the 1990s, and this trend has continued since 2000.

Lastly, we review the trend of poverty conditions in India. Figure 8.4 illustrates the population group-wise distribution of poor people, measured by the percentage of the population below the poverty line.[4] This figure shows that while the poverty ratio unanimously declined between FY 1973 and FY 1999, it began to increase between FY 1999 and FY 2004 in both rural and urban areas. Throughout the entire period, with the exception of FY 1993, the poverty ratio in rural areas was consistently higher than that in urban areas. However, in terms of the change rate, on average, rural areas showed a larger reduction in the poverty ratio than urban areas.

---

[4] In FY 2004, there were two types of measurements for population below the poverty line: the Uniform Reference Period (URP) and the Mixed Reference Period (MRP). In this study, we use a poverty ratio based on the URP.

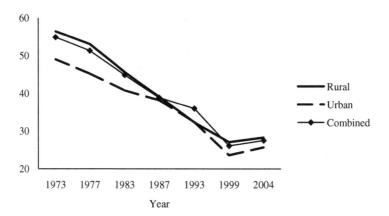

Figure 8.4   Population Group-wise Distribution of Percentage of Population below the Poverty Line (% of Persons)

Sources: RBI (2009) and Indiastat.com (http://www.indiastat.com/).

To sum up, financial inclusion in India was encouraged mainly in rural areas until the late 1980s. As the figures show, however, metropolitan areas have since experienced a significant bump in financial inclusion in terms of both access to and usage of financial services. These structural changes are considered to reflect the government's policy changes toward the banking sector as well as the environment surrounding commercial banks. On the other hand, with regard to poverty conditions, it was found that the poverty headcount ratio, having been in decline since FY 1973, began to increase between FY 1999 and FY 2004 in both rural and urban areas. According to data from the AIDIS, the share of household debt owed to non-institutional sources increased between 1991 and 2002, especially in rural areas. Therefore, the trend of the poverty ratio is generally in line with that of household debt.

8.4   Literature Review

The relationship between financial development and economic growth has received much attention in a large amount of the literature. From a theoretical viewpoint, some economists argue that more developed financial systems assist in mobilizing savings, facilitating investment, and promoting growth, whereas others propose that economic growth creates additional demands on financial services, which in turn may bring about more developed financial systems (Shan and Morris, 2002, p. 154). Besides, of late there has been an increased interest in the relationship between financial development, poverty reduction, and income inequality (e.g., Jalilian and Kirkpatrick, 2002; Clarke *et al.*, 2006; Beck *et al.*, 2007a; and so on). As this chapter pays special attention to financial inclusion, in this section, we survey the relevant prior studies for the link between financial inclusion and either economic growth or poverty reduction.

To begin with, Beck *et al.* (2007b) provided a set of banking sector outreach indicators and then analyzed the determinants of the proposed indicators. To indicate access to financial services, they presented data on the number of branches and automated teller machines per capita and per square kilometer. They also presented data on the number of loan and deposit accounts per capita and the average loan and deposit size relative to gross domestic product (GDP) per capita to measure the actual use of credit and deposit services. After verifying the validity of the outreach indicators, they explored the empirical association between them and an array of variables previously found to affect financial sector depth. Using a broad cross-section, including India, they found that the outreach indicators are significantly determined by per capita GDP, quality of governance, credit information environment, and communications infrastructure.

The RBI (2008) also empirically examined the relationship between financial inclusion and economic growth in general and infrastructure development. This was based in particular on state-wise data for 9 Indian states for the period 2001 to 2006. Here, the savings and credit accounts per 100 persons were used as proxy indicators of financial inclusion, while per capita income was taken as an indicator of economic growth. Electricity consumption in milliwatts per 100,000 persons and road lengths in kilometers were used to measure infrastructure development. The empirical results indicated that there is a two-way relationship between financial inclusion and economic and infrastructure developments. That is, financial inclusion has a positive effect on economic growth, while economic growth and infrastructure development seem to promote financial inclusion.

Burgess and Pande (2005) evaluated the importance of the state-led branch expansion program in India by examining its impact on the poverty ratio in rural and urban areas. They stated that due to the introduction of the new branch licensing policy in 1977, rural branch expansion was relatively higher in financially less developed states between 1977 and

1990, and that the reverse was true both before 1977 and after 1990. Based on these observations and using panel data for 16 states for the period 1961 to 2000, they empirically analyzed how the increase in the number of branches in rural unbanked locations affected the poverty headcount ratio. They reported that when evaluated at the sample mean, rural branch expansion could explain a 14.0 to 17.0 percentage point decline in the rural poverty headcount ratio, but it did not affect urban poverty.

Finally, Bhandari (2009) measured progress toward financial inclusion in India in the form of growth in deposit bank accounts and calculated Spearman's rank correlation between the state-wise growth in bank accounts and the percentage changes in the below-poverty line population. Using the data from FY 1999 and FY 2004 for Indian states and union territories, Bhandari found that while changes in the poverty ratio and the growth of bank accounts were negatively correlated in both rural and urban areas, the coefficients were statistically insignificant. Therefore, he concluded that the provision of banking services to the maximum number of people is unsuccessful as a poverty reduction strategy.

As mentioned above, the reviewed literature measured the extent of financial inclusion from data relating to the banking sector, such as the number of branches, the number of credit and deposit accounts, and/or the amounts of credit and deposits. We utilize the numbers of bank branches and bank accounts to assess both the extent of access to and usage of formal financial services. This differs from the reviewed literature, such as Burgess and Pande (2005), RBI (2008), and Bhandari (2009), which used either the number of bank branches or the number of bank accounts as the measure of financial inclusion. Among the reviewed literature, Beck *et al.* (2007b) used all the relevant variables to measure the degree of financial inclusion and explored its relation to per capita GDP, institutional quality, credit information environment, and so on. Unlike Beck *et al.* (2007b), we apply each of the financial inclusion measures to find their impact on poverty reduction in India.

8.5 Models and Data

This section provides a brief explanation of the empirical models as well as the definitions and sources of the variables. In our empirical analysis, we consider models in which the poverty headcount ratios for urban and rural areas are explained by the proxy for financial inclusion and control variables, including international openness, inflation rate, and output level. In estimating the models, we apply the dynamic generalized method of moments (GMM) estimator to unbalanced panel data for 25 states and union territories covering seven time periods between FY 1973 and FY 2004 (1973, 1977, 1983, 1987, 1993, 1999, and 2004).[5,6] Our models are as follows:

Model 1:

$$POVRU_{it} = \lambda POVRU_{i,t-1} + \beta_{i0} + \beta_{i1} FI_{it} + \beta_{i2} OPEN_t$$
$$+ \beta_{i3} INF_t + \beta_{i4} Y_{it} + u_{it}, \tag{1}$$

Model 2:

$$POVUR_{it} = \lambda POVUR_{i,t-1} + \beta_{i0} + \beta_{i1} FI_{it} + \beta_{i2} OPEN_t$$
$$+ \beta_{i3} INF_t + \beta_{i4} Y_{it} + u_{it}, \tag{2}$$

where $POVRU_{it}$ is the poverty headcount ratio in rural areas for region i at time t, $POVUR_{it}$ is the poverty headcount ratio in urban areas for region i at time t, FI_{it} is a proxy for financial inclusion for region i at time t, $OPEN_t$ is the sum of exports and imports as a share of the country's GDP at time t, INF_t is the country's inflation rate at time t, Y_{it} is the output of region i at time t, u_{it} is the error term, $i(= 1, 2, \ldots, N)$ is the number of cross-sections, and $t(= 1, 2, \ldots, T)$ is the number of time series (see Table 8.3 for more precise definitions).

The poverty headcount ratios (*POVRU* and *POVUR*) are measured by using the percentage of the population below the poverty line set by the Indian government. The data are obtained from RBI (2009) and the Web sites of the Planning Commission and Indiastat.com.

---

[5]The 25 states and union territories covered in this study are as follows: Andhra Pradesh, Arunachal Pradesh, Assam, Bihar, Gujarat, Haryana, Himachal Pradesh, Jammu & Kashmir, Karnataka, Kerala, Madhya Pradesh, Maharashtra, Manipur, Meghalaya, Nagaland, Odisha, Punjab, Rajasthan, Tamil Nadu, Tripura, West Bengal, Andaman & Nicobar Islands, Chandigarh, Delhi, and Puducherry.

[6]All benchmark years are fiscal years, except for 1983, which is the calendar year.

Table 8.3 Definition and Sources of Each Variable

Variables	Definition	Sources
POVRU	The percentage of the population below the poverty line set by the Indian government in rural areas.	RBI (2009) and the Web sites of the Planning Commission (http:// planningcommission.gov.in/) and Indiastat.com (http://www. indiastat.com/default.aspx).
POVUR	The percentage of the population below the poverty line set by the Indian government in urban areas.	
*FI*1	The state-wise number of scheduled commercial bank branches divided by the population of each state multiplied by 10,000.	Various issues of Banking Statistics and Basic Statistical Returns of Scheduled Commercial Banks in India published by the RBI (State-wise population from RBI (2009)).
*FI*2	The state-wise number of deposit accounts divided by the population of each state.	
*FI*3	The state-wise number of credit accounts divided by the population of each state.	
OPEN	The sum of exports and imports as a share of nominal GDP.	RBI (2009)
INF	Inflation rate throughout India calculated from the WPI (%).	
Y	The log of NSDP at constant prices (base: FY 1999).	

Financial inclusion (*FI*) is measured by three variables: the number of bank branches (*FI*1), the number of credit accounts (*FI*2), and the number of deposit accounts (*FI*3) of the region's scheduled commercial banks divided by the population in each region.[7] The number of bank branches is a proxy for physical access to financial services, and the other criteria are indicative of the actual use of formal financial services. The data are obtained from various issues of Banking Statistics and Basic Statistical Returns of Scheduled Commercial Banks in India published by the RBI. Since the primary objective of financial inclusion is to alleviate poverty

[7]We multiply *FI*1 by 10,000 in order to adjust the unit in our empirical analysis, i.e., *FI*1 is equal to the ratio of the number of bank branches multiplied by 10,000 to the population.

conditions by promoting the provision of financial services, we expect financial inclusion to be associated with a lower poverty ratio.

Models 1 and 2 also include control variables to avoid any possible omitted variables. They are two sets of factors: macroeconomic and regional environments. For the macroeconomic environment, we consider international openness (*OPEN*) and inflation rate (*INF*). For the regional environment, we consider the output of each region (*Y*). These variables are taken from RBI (2009). We assume that a higher income level has a positive impact on poverty reduction, whereas international openness and higher inflation have adverse impacts on the poor.

8.6 Empirical Results

Since the explanatory variables include the lagged value of the explained variable, we cannot apply the ordinary regression techniques. Instead, we estimate each model using the dynamic panel GMM estimators developed by Arellano and Bond (1991), so that we can also deal with the endogeneity problem.[8]

Table 8.4 reports the empirical results of the GMM estimations. The first two columns report the regression results of Models 1 and 2 using the number of bank branches (*FI*1) as the measure of financial inclusion. In both regressions, the coefficients on *FI*1 are significantly estimated to be negative; this suggests that easier access to formal financial services has a positive impact on poverty alleviation in both rural and urban areas. This is partly consistent with the findings of Burgess and Pande (2005), who stated that branch expansion can explain the decline in the rural poverty ratio, but does not affect urban poverty. With regard to the control variables, the results also show that the coefficients on *OPEN*, *INF*, and *Y* in both areas are statistically significant with the expected signs.

Next, Columns 3 to 6 display the results of the regression using either the number of deposit accounts (*FI*2) or the number of credit accounts (*FI*3) as the measure of financial inclusion. The empirical results show

---

[8]For each model, the poverty ratio is used as the dynamic instrumental variable, while the openness measure, inflation rate, and regional output are used as the standard instrumental variables.

Table 8.4   Empirical Results

	1	2	3	4	5	6
POVRU(−1)	0.276 (0.000)***		0.330 (0.000)***		0.322 (0.000)***	
POVUR(−1)		0.127 (0.000)***		0.012 (0.703)		0.069 (0.161)
*FI*1	−20.616 (0.000)***	−10.555 (0.000)***				
*FI*2			−5.829 (0.056)*	−13.008 (0.000)***		
*FI*3					13.568 (0.461)	−42.927 (0.001)***
OPEN	12.064 (0.064)*	46.295 (0.000)***	43.933 (0.000)***	40.834 (0.000)***	61.854 (0.000)***	59.023 (0.000)***
INF	179.281 (0.000)***	83.482 (0.000)***	58.222 (0.012)**	87.636 (0.003)***	12.922 (0.733)	71.722 (0.037)**
Y	−31.263 (0.000)***	−40.218 (0.000)***	−39.934 (0.000)***	−39.956 (0.000)***	−49.888 (0.000)***	−45.536 (0.000)***
J-statistic	23.804 (0.162)	21.017 (0.279)	23.913 (0.158)	20.269 (0.318)	23.091 (0.187)	20.992 (0.280)
Number of Observations	115	115	115	115	115	115

Notes: (1) Numbers in parentheses are *p*-values.
(2) Significance at the 1%, 5%, and 10% level is indicated by ***, **, and *, respectively.
(3) The dependent variable is the poverty ratio. *POVRU* is the poverty ratio in rural areas, and *POVUR*, in urban areas. *FI*1 is equal to the number of bank branches of the region's scheduled commercial banks divided by the population in each region. *FI*2 and *FI*3 are equal to the number of credit accounts and the number of deposit accounts respectively of the region's scheduled commercial banks divided by the population in each region. *OPEN* is the ratio of exports plus imports to GDP. *INF* is equal to the growth rate of the WPI. *Y* is the logarithm of output in each state.

that the coefficients of deposit accounts in both areas and credit accounts in urban areas are significantly estimated to be negative, while the coefficient of credit accounts in rural areas is positive, but becomes insignificant, as shown in Column 5. These results suggest that the improved usage of financial services in the form of bank accounts generally reduces the poverty ratio in both rural and urban areas; however, this does not apply for credit accounts in rural areas. This is in contrast to the results of Bhandari (2009), wherein changes in the poverty ratio and the growth in deposit accounts were insignificantly correlated, although the methodologies employed are different. Concerning the control variables, the results are the same as those in the first two columns, except for *INF* in Column 5, which is now statistically insignificant.

Finally, Table 8.4 reports the J-statistic and its associated p-value for each model. The J-statistic is used as a test of over-identifying moment conditions. As is clear from the table, the over-identifying restriction cannot be rejected at the 5% significance level, and thus the model specification is empirically supported.

In summation, Table 8.4 indicates that, in general, financial inclusion variables, excluding the number of credit accounts in rural areas, have a significant negative association with the poverty ratio in both rural and urban areas. Considering the results of each component of the financial inclusion variables, it is suggested that easier access to and greater use of formal financial services have had a positive impact on poverty alleviation throughout India.

8.7 Concluding Remarks

Financial inclusion is generally defined as the process of ensuring access to and usage of basic formal financial services to all people at an affordable cost. In India, there have been various measures taken to encourage financial inclusion since the late 1960s. Although new measures in the form of microfinance, such as the SBLP, have been implemented as a result of economic liberalization since the early 1990s, commercial banks still play a pivotal role in the promotion of financial inclusion in India. Accordingly, in this chapter, after reviewing the relevant data, we analyzed whether financial inclusion measures have a statistically significant relationship with poverty conditions by estimating panel data regression models.

According to the relevant data on commercial banks, financial inclusion in India was encouraged mainly in rural areas until the late 1980s, but subsequently, metropolitan areas experienced a significant bump in financial inclusion. On the other hand, with regard to poverty conditions, it was found that the poverty headcount ratio, having been in decline since FY 1973, began to increase between FY 1999 and FY 2004 in both rural and urban areas.

For empirical analysis, we used unbalanced panel data for 25 states and union territories covering seven time periods between FY 1973 and FY 2004. The model was specified to examine the impact of financial inclusion on poverty reduction. Following the relevant literature, the number of bank branches was regarded as the measure of physical access to financial services, while the number of bank accounts was used as the measure of usage of financial services. The econometric results showed that excluding the number of credit accounts in rural areas, these variables have a statistically significant negative relationship with the poverty ratio in rural and urban areas, even when controlling for international openness, inflation rate, and output. Accordingly, since our results suggest that both access to and usage of financial services have actually contributed toward alleviating poverty conditions throughout India, it is desirable that Indian policymakers continue their efforts to push forward financial inclusion vigorously and strengthen socio-financial safety net for the poor.

In this study, we attempted to focus on the relationship between financial inclusion measures on the one hand and the poverty ratio on the other. However, these measures make up only one part of basic financial services, and thus may only partially reflect the degree of financial inclusion in a country. It is necessary to develop new indicators to measure financial inclusion from different viewpoints. In addition, although we have examined the direct link between financial inclusion and the poverty ratio, the relevant literature indicates that finance could serve to relieve poverty through a variety of routes. Therefore, more work will be needed to re-examine the link between financial inclusion and the poverty ratio by considering relevant variables, especially income distribution.

References

Arellano, M., Bond, S., 1991. Some tests of specification for panel data: Monte Carlo evidence and an application to employment equations. *Review of Economic Studies* 58, 277–297.

Beck, T., Demirgüç-Kunt, A., Levine, R., 2007a. Finance, inequality and the poor. *Journal of Economic Growth* 12, 27–49.

Beck, T., Demirgüç-Kunt, A., Martinez Peria, M.S., 2007b. Reaching out: Access to and use of banking services across countries. *Journal of Financial Economics* 85, 234–266.

Bhandari, A.K., 2009. Access to banking services and poverty reduction: A statewise assessment in India. IZA Discussion Paper 4132, Institute for the Study of Labor, Bonn.

Burgess, R., Pande, R., 2005. Do rural banks matter? Evidence from the Indian social banking experiment. *American Economic Review* 95, 780–795.

Chavan, P., 2007. Access to bank credit: Implications for Dalit rural households. *Economic and Political Weekly* 42, 3219–3224.

Claessens, S., 2005. Access to financial services: A review of the issues and public policy objectives. World Bank Policy Research Working Paper 3589, The World Bank, Washington, DC.

Clarke, G., Xu, L.C., Zou, H-F., 2006. Finance and income inequality: What do the data tell us? *Southern Economic Journal* 72, 578–596.

Jalilian, H., Kirkpatrick, C., 2002. Financial development and poverty reduction in developing countries. *International Journal of Finance & Economics* 7, 97–108.

Joshi, D.P., 2006. *Social Banking: Promise, Performance and Potential.* Foundation Books, New Delhi.

Leeladhar, V., 2006. Taking banking services to the common man — Financial inclusion. *RBI Monthly Bulletin January*, Reserve Bank of India, Mumbai, 73–77.

Leeladhar, V., 2008. The Indian banking industry — A retrospect of select aspects. *RBI Monthly Bulletin September*, Reserve Bank of India, Mumbai, 1501–1510.

National Sample Survey Organization (NSSO), 1998a. *Indebtedness of Rural Households as on 30.6.1991: Debt and Investment Survey*, no. 420. NSSO, New Delhi.

National Sample Survey Organization (NSSO), 1998b. *Indebtedness of Urban Households as on 30.6.1991: Debt and Investment Survey*, no. 421. NSSO, New Delhi.

National Sample Survey Organization (NSSO), 2005. *Household Indebtedness in India as on 30.06.2002; All India Debt and Investment Survey*, no. 501. NSSO. New Delhi.

Rao, K.G.K.S., 2007. Financial inclusion: An introspection. *Economic and Political Weekly* 42, 355–360.

Reserve Bank of India (RBI), 1965. All India rural debt and investment survey, 1961–62. *RBI Monthly Bulletin September*, RBI, Mumbai, 1296–1393.

Reserve Bank of India (RBI), 1977. Indebtedness of Rural Households and Availability of Institutional Finance. *All India Debt and Investment Survey 1971–72.* RBI, Mumbai.

Reserve Bank of India (RBI), 1987. *All India Debt and Investment Survey, 1981–82: Assets and Liabilities of Households as on 30th June 1981.* RBI, Mumbai.

Reserve Bank of India (RBI), 1999. *Annual Report 1998–99.* RBI, Mumbai.

Reserve Bank of India (RBI), 2005. *Annual Policy Statement for the Year 2005–06.* RBI, Mumbai.

Reserve Bank of India (RBI), 2008. *Financial inclusion, in: Report on Currency and Finance 2007–08.* RBI, Mumbai, pp. 294–348.

Reserve Bank of India (RBI), 2009. *Handbook on Statistics of Indian Economy 2008–09.* RBI, Mumbai.

Reserve Bank of India (RBI), 2012. *Annual Report 2011–12.* RBI, Mumbai.

Reserve Bank of India (RBI), various issues. *Banking Statistics: Basic Statistical Returns.* RBI, Mumbai.

Reserve Bank of India (RBI), various issues. *Basic Statistical Returns of Scheduled Commercial Banks in India.* RBI, Mumbai.

Sen, K., Vaidya, R.R., 1997. *The Process of Financial Liberalization.* Oxford University Press, Delhi.

Shajahan, K.M., 1998. Priority sector bank lending: Some important issues. *Economic and Political Weekly* 33, 2749–2756.

Shan, J., Morris, A., 2002. Does financial development 'lead' economic growth? *International Review of Applied Economics* 16, 153–168.

Subbarao, D., 2010. Financial inclusion: Challenges and opportunities. *RBI Monthly Bulletin January*, Reserve Bank of India, Mumbai, 1–10.

Chapter 9

Concluding Remarks: Monetary Policy and Financial Sector for Sustainable Economic Growth and Poverty Reduction

The objectives of monetary policy in India have been generally interpreted as related to price stability and economic growth, and they have remained unchanged since the enactment of the Reserve Bank of India (RBI) Act in 1934. In contrast, monetary policy procedures have undergone significant changes in India, as reflected by the process of financial sector reforms, which began in the early 1990s. Part 1 of this book composed of Chapters 1–3 focused on the transition of India's monetary policy frameworks, and conducted an empirical analysis on the effectiveness of policy frameworks in the past, present and expected future, that is, monetary targeting, the multiple indicator approach (MIA), and inflation targeting, respectively.

In 1998, the RBI formally announced a shift in its policy framework from monetary targeting, focused on the growth of the broad monetary aggregate M3 as the intermediate target, to the MIA, wherein movements not only in M3, but also in a host of other macroeconomic variables are tracked for policy responses. This shift was partly prompted by the apprehension that the money demand function had become unstable as a result of financial innovations and financial sector reforms relative to the past. In order to elucidate the validity of such apprehension, in Chapter 1 we examined the long-run stability and the characteristics of India's money demand function by applying cointegration test and the dynamic ordinary least squares (DOLS) method. The results indicated that the money demand function is stable when monetary aggregate is defined as M1 or M2, but no such relation is observed when monetary aggregate is defined as M3.

These results were obtained using both monthly data from 1980 to 2007 and annual data from 1976 to 2007.

Since 1998, under the MIA, the RBI has considered a variety of macroeconomic variables as policy indicators, and has focused on their movements to draw future perspectives for policy objectives. In Chapter 2, we empirically analyzed which policy indicator has actually served as an information variable under the current monetary policy framework. For this purpose, we examined the causal relationships of each macroeconomic variable the RBI monitors as policy indicators with both output and price levels from 1998 to 2009 by applying the Granger causality test based on the vector autoregression (VAR) model. Empirical results showed that except for bank credit, all indicator variables considered in this analysis have a causal relationship with either output or price level, suggesting that most preannounced macroeconomic variables are useful in predicting the movements of policy objectives. On subdividing monetary aggregates, M1 and M2 are found to Granger-cause output, whereas M3 causes neither output nor price level.

Even after the shift of monetary policy framework from monetary targeting to the MIA, the RBI still reports the growth rate forecast for M3 in its policy statement and regards it as the principal measure of future price movements. However, based on our empirical results in Chapters 1 and 2, it is recommended that the Indian central bank should utilize the information content of M1 and M2, rather than M3, for monetary policy formulation.

Towards the end of Part 1, Chapter 3 estimated the Taylor rule-type reaction function for India by applying the DOLS to examine the effect of short-term interest rate on inflation rate. Empirical results using monthly data from 1998 to 2009 indicated that India's monetary policy could respond appropriately to internal supply–demand gaps but not to changes in price level. In other words, short-term interest rate is not yet an effective instrument to control inflation rate, suggesting that India has failed to meet one of the key preconditions for inflation targeting. Accordingly, based on the empirical results, it has been concluded that the RBI is not ready to focus more on the inflation rate, let alone adopt an inflation-targeting type policy framework.

In relation with monetary policy, we also analyzed exchange rate policy in India. First, in Chapter 3, we estimated the augmented Taylor rule with exchange rate as the objective variable. This led us to find that the exchange rate coefficient was statistically significant and that its sign condition was consistent with theoretical rationale, which implies a relatively high interest rate when the exchange rate depreciates and a relatively low interest rate when the real exchange rate appreciates.

Chapter 6 analyzed the sources of real and nominal exchange rate fluctuations in India by employing the structural VAR model and using monthly data from 1999 to 2009. The VAR system consists of three variables: the nominal exchange rate, the real exchange rate, and the relative output of India and a foreign country. The empirical evidence demonstrated that real shocks are the main sources of fluctuations in both real and nominal exchange rates, suggesting that the central bank cannot maintain the exchange rate at its desired level in the long run.

In developing countries like India, it is natural for policymakers to pay considerable attention to exchange rate movements since the exchange rate has a substantial impact on export price competitiveness. However, our results in Chapter 3 and Chapter 6 indicated that although the RBI attempts to respond to developments in the foreign exchange market, it cannot affect exchange rate movements. In the wake of economic globalization, India is increasingly exposed to abrupt and large-scale fluctuations in exchange rate. Therefore, Indian policymakers are required to monitor the exchange rate more closely and take preemptive measures against large currency fluctuations.

Part 2 of this book considered the Indian financial markets undergoing phenomenal growth over the last decade. In addition to foreign exchange market in Chapter 6, the stock market has been discussed in Chapter 4 and the commodity market in Chapter 5.

In Chapter 4, pertaining to the stock market in India, we examined the causalities in the mean and the variance between stock returns and foreign institutional investment (FII) in Indian equities by applying the cross-correlation function (CCF) approach. The sample period from January 1999 to March 2008 was divided into two sub-sample periods before and after May 2003, when net FII inflows and stock price index followed significant upward trends. The results of the CCF approach indicated that the causality from stock returns to FII flows exists in both sample periods, whereas the causality from FII flows to stock returns exists only in the latter period, implying that FII flows influenced the movement of Indian stock prices during the more recent sample period.

Chapter 5 analyzed the market efficiency hypothesis of the commodity futures market in India. We conducted the Johansen cointegration test for multi-commodity spot and futures price indices from January 2006 to March 2011, and then tested the unbiasedness hypothesis by examining whether the two price indices have a cointegrating vector $(1, -1)$. We found that the unbiasedness hypothesis is rejected for the entire sample period. However, on dividing the sample period into three sub-samples, the unbiasedness hypothesis is not rejected for the more recent sample period. In India, the total value of commodities traded has shown significant growth since 2008, and the commodity price indices have also increased since mid-2009. Therefore, this chapter implies that as the market size expands, the commodity futures market becomes efficient in that the futures price generally operates as an unbiased predictor of the spot price.

As stated in Part 2, the Indian financial markets have witnessed significant changes in the recent years. In line with economic growth, these markets are expected to expand their scale and complicate the transaction forms. Therefore, the Indian authorities will be required to further improve institutional infrastructure to ensure that expanding and deepening financial markets contribute to economic growth.

As with economic growth, poverty reduction is another crucial problem for India to resolve. Despite remarkable economic growth in recent years, India is home to a large number of poor. Part 3 of this book examined the role of financial development for poverty alleviation in India from two different perspectives.

First, in Chapter 7, we empirically analyzed whether financial deepening is conducive to poverty reduction. Financial deepening is typically defined as an increase in the proportion of the financial sector to the real sector, and is believed to help reduce poverty, not only directly, but also indirectly through its effect on economic growth, by eliminating credit constraints on the poor, and increasing their productive assets and productivity. In our empirical analysis, we considered models in which the poverty headcount ratio is explained by financial deepening and a set of control variables, and estimated the models by using unbalanced state-level panel data from FY 1973 to FY 2004. We measured financial depth by the credit amount or deposit amount of the scheduled commercial banks, since they play a dominant role in the Indian financial sector. From the generalized method of moments (GMM) estimations, we found that financial deepening displays a significant positive effect on poverty alleviation. Recently, an increasing number of empirical analyses on large samples of countries have reached a consensus that financial deepening is effective in alleviating poverty. Therefore, it appears that the findings derived in the context of a large sample of countries can also be applied in the case of a specific country, India.

Chapter 8 examined whether and to what extent financial inclusion — the increased use of and access to financial services among poor people — contributes to poverty alleviation in India. In this chapter, we measured the degree of financial inclusion by applying three indicators related to commercial banks: the number of branches, the number of credit accounts, and the number of deposit accounts, and estimated the models in which the poverty ratio is explained by each indicator of financial inclusion and certain control variables by using unbalanced state-level panel data from FY 1973 to FY 2004. The empirical results of the GMM estimations show that financial inclusion variables, excluding the number of credit accounts in rural areas, have a significant negative association with the poverty ratio in both rural and urban areas. In India, a large number of poor continue to remain unbanked, especially in rural areas, and policy effort still has a long way to go to advance financial inclusion. Based on the conclusion of this chapter, it is desirable that Indian policymakers continue their efforts to push forward financial inclusion vigorously and strengthen socio-financial safety net for the poor.

In summary, each chapter indicates that India has made significant progress on monetary and financial issues during the recent growth phase. In order to promote further economic growth, India will be required to communicate appropriately with the financial markets and improve the environment for well-developed financial markets. Moreover, in order to realize sustainable economic growth, poverty reduction is essential for India because economic growth with rising income inequality could result in disproportional distribution of the benefits of growth, leading to social unrest. Therefore, the Indian authorities will also be required to achieve economic growth for poverty reduction by accelerating financial development in terms of scale, accessibility, and availability.

Index

Ace Derivatives and Commodity Exchange, 73
All India Debt and Investment Survey (AIDIS), 131–132, 136
AR-exponential GARCH (AR-EGARCH), 64–65

balance of payments crisis, 9
bank nationalization, 128
Bombay Stock Exchange (BSE) SENSEX 30, 53, 61
branch licensing policy, 128–129, 134, 137

cash reserve ratio (CRR), 10, 27–29
causality, 32, 36, 57, 59, 62–63, 71, 76, 101, 105–106, 149
    causality in mean, 58–60, 65, 69, 71
    causality in variance, 58, 60–61, 65, 69, 71
    Granger causality, 2, 29–31, 55–57, 62–63, 71, 105–106, 148
commodity futures, 2–3, 73–77, 80, 82–83, 150
cross-correlation function (CCF), 2, 55, 58, 60, 64–65, 71, 149

financial deepening, 3–4, 102–106, 108–110, 113, 117–119, 121–122, 127, 150–151
financial (sector) depth, 4, 104, 106, 137, 150
financial development, 1, 3–4, 101–106, 108, 111, 113, 127, 136–137, 150–151

financial inclusion, 4, 122, 127–134, 136–141, 143–144, 151
foreign direct investment, 56, 110–115
foreign institutional investment (FII), 2, 53–58, 61–65, 69, 71–72, 149–150
foreign (institutional) investors, 2, 53–54, 56–57, 71
Forward Markets Commission (FMC), 73

General Credit Card, 122, 130
Generalized Autoregressive Conditional Heteroscedasticity (GARCH), 64–65
generalized method of moments (GMM), 40–41, 105, 141, 151
    dynamic (panel) GMM, 106, 113, 119, 139, 141
Gini coefficient, 104, 111
Government of India (GOI) (Indian government), 3–4, 39, 53, 73, 83, 88, 102, 108, 122, 139

inclusive growth, 4, 102, 122
inflation targeting, 10, 39, 48, 147–148
information variable, 28, 30, 35–36, 148
intermediate target(s), 1, 10, 24, 28, 32, 36, 147
International Monetary Fund (IMF), 14, 32, 42, 89

Kisan Credit Cards (KCCs), 130
know-your-customer procedure, 122, 131

liquidity adjustment facility (LAF), 27, 28
Lok Sabha, 61

marginal standing facility (MSF), 28
market efficiency, 3, 75–76, 81–82, 150
monetary aggregate(s), 10, 14, 29, 32–34, 36, 106, 147–148
   monetary policy framework(s), 2, 28, 30, 32, 34–35, 147–148
   monetary policy reaction function, 2, 39–41, 46, 48
   monetary policy rule(s), 40–41, 48
monetary (supply) targeting, 1–2, 10, 24, 28, 32–36, 147–148
money demand, 1, 11–13, 24, 28
   money demand function(s), 2, 10–17, 19–24, 28, 147
Multi Commodity Exchange of India (MCX), 73, 76, 78, 82
   MCXCOMDEX, 78
   MCXSCOMDEX, 78
multiple indicator approach (MIA), 2, 10, 24, 28–32, 35–36, 39, 147–148

National Commodity and Derivatives Exchange (NCDEX), 73, 76
National Multi Commodity Exchange of India, 73
National Sample Survey Organization (NSSO), 108, 131
"no-frills" banking account, 122, 130
nominal effective exchange rate (NEER), 87

operating instruments, 10, 24, 27
operating target, 28
ordinary least squares (OLS), 15, 31, 40–41, 43, 63, 77
   dynamic OLS (DOLS), 2–3, 11, 13, 15–16, 19, 22, 41, 44–48, 75, 77–78, 80–82, 147–148
   fully modified OLS (FMOLS), 3, 41, 43–48, 75, 77–78, 80–82

policy indicator(s), 2, 28–29, 31–33, 35–36, 148
portfolio investment(s), 53, 55–56, 69
poverty line, 102, 108, 135, 138–139
poverty (head count) ratio(s), 3, 102–105, 108, 110, 112–121, 128, 135–139, 141–144, 150–151
priority sector lending, 128–129

real effective exchange rate (REER), 30, 40–43, 46–47, 87, 95
reference indicator, 24
Regional Rural Banks (RRBs), 128–130
repo and reverse repo, 28, 39
Reserve Bank of India (RBI), 1–3, 9–10, 13–14, 24, 27–36, 39, 42, 48, 56, 71, 87, 95–96, 106, 108–109, 111, 122, 127–131, 133, 137–141, 147–149
Reserve Bank of India (RBI) Act, 27, 106, 147

scheduled (commercial) bank(s), 4, 28, 106, 109, 112, 119, 121, 129, 133, 140, 150
Securities and Exchange Board of India (SEBI), 61
Self-Help Group (SHG)-Bank Linkage Program (SBLP), 129–130, 143
statutory liquidity ratio (SLR), 10

Taylor rule, 2, 40–41, 45–46, 48, 148

vector autoregression (VAR), 2–3, 29–31, 62–63, 89, 91–92, 94, 148–149
   bivariate VAR, 88
   bivariate structural VAR, 57
   lag-augmented VAR (LA-VAR), 30–31, 36, 55, 62–63, 71
   structural VAR (SVAR), 29, 89, 92, 149
   trivariate VAR, 32, 89, 95

Printed in the United States
By Bookmasters